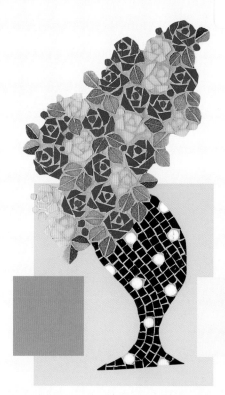

THE MOSAIC ARTIST'S SOURCEBOOK

THE MOSAIC ARTIST'S SOURCEBOOK

TERESA MILLS

APPLE

A QUARTO BOOK

First published in the United Kingdom
by Apple Press
7 Greenland Street
London
NW1 0ND
www.apple-press.com

Reprinted 2006, 2008 (twice)

ISBN: 978-1-84543-000-9

QUAR.MAB

Conceived, designed and produced by
Quarto Publishing plc
The Old Brewery
6 Blundell Street
London N7 9BH

Project Editor **Gillian Haslam**
Art Editor **Sheila Volpe**
Designer **Karin Skånberg**
Photographer **Martin Norris**
Illustrator **Kuo Kang Chen**
Indexer **Angela Airey**
Picture Researcher **Claudia Tate**
Assistant Art director **Penny Cobb**

Art Director **Moira Clinch**
Publisher **Piers Spence**

Manufactured by Universal Graphics, Singapore
Printed by Midas Printing International Limited, China

9 8 7 6 5 4

To Sam, Oscar, and Paul, and to
my Mum and Dad

CONTENTS

INTRODUCTION

Mosaic is an art form with a long history that has produced many wonderful works of decorative art. It was the ancient Greeks, and then the Romans to whom they passed their skills, who developed the technique of using small fragments of stone, ceramics and then glass to create pictures and patterns.

Thousands of years ago, these civilizations developed the materials and the designs which remain the foundation of mosaic art and which are often copied but seldom surpassed. The Romans spread the art form across their empire, leaving hundreds of examples of mosaics that can still be seen today in the remains of their public buildings and

homes. A second great flowering of mosaic art took place and spread from the Eastern Mediterranean during the Byzantine period from the fifth century onwards, with perhaps the finest

examples still surviving in Ravenna, Italy.

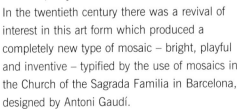

In the twentieth century there was a revival of interest in this art form which produced a completely new type of mosaic – bright, playful and inventive – typified by the use of mosaics in the Church of the Sagrada Familia in Barcelona, designed by Antoni Gaudí.

Yet, whilst mosaic has an illustrious history, it is also an art form accessible to anyone with the perseverance to master the skill of cutting tiles and with the patience to carefully lay out and glue down the constituent parts of a design. This book's aim is to help you discover and develop the skills and patience that mosaic work requires. In the following pages you will find an explanation of the basic mosaic techniques, followed by a vast selection of motifs and patterns that vary in their degree of difficulty. Each design is provided in outline form on a grid to allow you to copy and scale it to the size you desire.

The drawings, however, are only a starting point. As you will see, you can combine elements of the motifs in any number of ways – such as combining borders with a central motif – whilst the possibilities available from using different colour combinations and fill-in effects are limitless.

My main hope for this book is that it will help you discover some of the joys of mosaic. Creating a mosaic is a hugely exciting process as you develop the design and experiment with the possibilities of shape and colour. Yet mosaicing can also be highly relaxing and therapeutic, as you patiently fill and extend areas of tiles. The satisfaction of seeing a picture taking shape, and

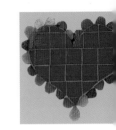

the final sense of revelation as you clean the grout from the tiles, remains a unique pleasure no matter how many pictures or designs you create. The luminosity of mosaic tiles and the ability of a material that is so hard and smooth to create designs that are soft and subtle will continue to amaze you. With their durability, and usefulness in decoration and in the creation of functional objects, mosaics have a tactile dimension like few other art forms.

If you get bitten by the mosaic bug, you will find yourself seeing possibilities for mosaics everywhere – even in the most common-or-garden object or pattern. You will catch yourself looking at paving stones, old walls, even the random shapes of pebbles and fallen leaves, to trace out new patterns and configurations for your tiles. You will also begin filing away magazine cuttings and postcards, scraps of fabric and wallpaper, and anything that one day might be a source for a picture. And, of course, you will always be on the look out for new and old tiles, pieces of broken crockery, and anything from shells to buttons that you can use in a mosaic.

I wish you well in all your endeavours in mosaics and hope that the bug bites you!

TERESA MILLS

HOW TO USE THIS BOOK

The materials you will need and the best tools for the job are described on pages 28–43. Turn to page 44 for core techniques, teaching the basic skills for transferring designs, scaling, cutting and assembly. The mosaic patterns are organized into themes, starting on page 76.

Scale drawing Each mosaic has a scale drawing for scaling up or down, by hand or on a photocopier or a computer scanner. Follow the instructions on page 52.

Introductory text The author has plenty of suggestions for how to vary the design, identifies the parts that require special skills, and suggests how the piece might be used in an interior setting.

Grading Each motif is graded according to degree of difficulty on a scale of 1–4. If you're a beginner, start with grade 1. The trickiest mosaics use the smallest tiles cut in intricate shapes.

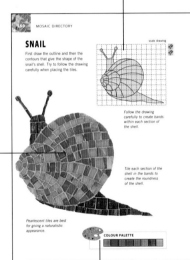

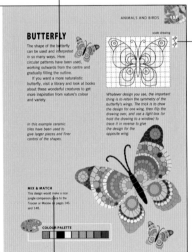

Photograph of mosaic A photograph of the finished mosaic design, showing the arrangement of tiles, making it easier to reproduce.

Colour palette This lists the colours used in the sample featured, but of course you can change the colour combinations to suit your taste or to match to a particular room decor.

Mix and match Some motifs lend themselves to being mixed with other motifs found elsewhere in the Directory. Relevant page references are given, so you can cross refer.

INSPIRATIONS

This chapter features a wide variety of finished pictures from some of the most accomplished artists working in the mosaic medium. The variety of different techniques and styles they use demonstrate how there is no right or wrong way to create original or exciting pieces of work. Mosaic art is a journey in which you are constantly discovering new things, and as you work on one piece you will discover new ideas to develop in your next piece of work. The pieces on the following pages are by artists who have taken that journey and, through their patience and dedication, created breathtaking pieces of work that can be an inspiration to all of us.

SUNFLOWERS
Sudarshan Deshmukh

This simple composition of overlapping sunflower heads is given vitality and movement through the vibrancy of the delicate shards that make up the flower heads, contrasted with the squarer, rolling tiles of the sky.

YELLOW TANG
Judy Wood

Fish provide a wonderful inspirational source for the mosaic artist with their endless variety of colours and shapes. Here, the careful cutting of the yellow tiles for the fins and scales provides a contrast to the flat, geometric red facial features.

UNDERWATER
Sudarshan Deshmukh

These undulating leaves seem to be held in the upward-flowing lines of the water, while the glass beads, which suggest bubbles, complete and add highlights to this delicate design.

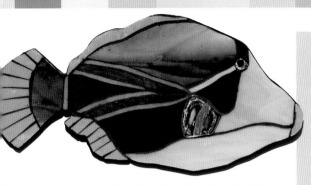

PICASSO TRIGGER FISH
Judy Wood

The large mosaic plates used here provide subtle gradation, creating the solidity of this fish's body. The geometric fan pattern of the tail suggests strength and movement.

ORNATE BUTTERFLY FISH
Judy Wood

The centre of this beautiful design is the strong, sweeping orange stripes rendered from single pieces of tile. The surrounding complementary blue adds to the luminescence of the orange, whilst the meticulous tiling of the fins and tail neatly frames the piece.

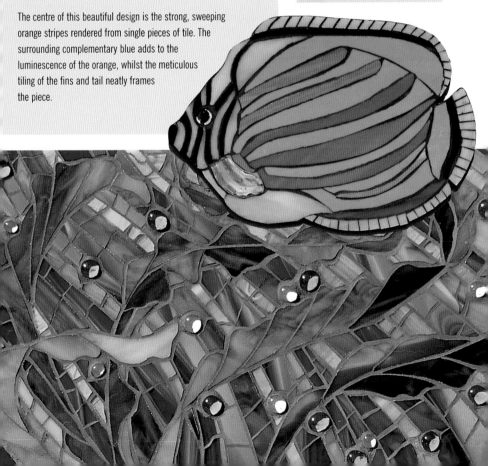

MAGPIE
Magnus Irvin

This striking composition is achieved by the unusually close-up viewpoint to the bird with its eye, leading to the suspended, almost threatening, hourglass. The finished effect is an ambiguous, almost surreal sense of puzzlement and menace.

FISH WITH GUILLOCHE
Jo Letchford

The curves of the waves are set off against the sharpness of the fish's spines and teeth. Using mosaic to create a picture frame is a useful device, in this case incorporating a classical motif.

REPTILES
Philippa Beveridge

This picture creates a classical trompe l'oeil effect: the pattern of the floor echoes the sinuous shape of the reptiles, while the use of shadow and the positioning of the lizards make them appear to be sitting on top of the picture frame.

CARPET MOSAIC
Rosalind Wates

This lovely mosaic gives the effect of a richly woven tapestry or carpet. A series of rich borders in subtle shades of blue and lilac surround a simply composed central panel of delightful floral and animal motifs.

ANIMALS, BIRDS AND INSECTS
Anna Wyner

This picture is mosaic on a grand scale, which achieves a highly elegant, almost classical effect. The rich golden palette and the formal positioning of the birds and animals in the landscape communicate an atmosphere which is both serene and disturbing at the same time.

PEACOCK
Irina Charny

This is an imaginative and unusual portrayal of a peacock with the key elements of the bird confined to a narrow strip. Even so, the picture still manages to suggest great depth between the head and tail of the bird and focuses attention on the detail of the plumage rather than the shape of the peacock.

ZEBRA
Judy Wood

This is another picture in which colours and patterns from the natural world provide inspiration for the mosaicist. Here, the stark black and white geometry of the zebra's coat has been counterpointed by the lush colours of the foliage and background that frame the animal's head.

ELEPHANT
Marcelo José de Melo

The broad shape of this African elephant's head makes it ideally suited for incorporation into a circular design. The even-sized and similarly toned tiles have been handled skilfully so the mosaic retains a unified effect, but without merging and losing the elements of the design.

HANDPRINT WAR PONY
Judy Wood

In this mosaic, the naturalistic elements of the horse's face almost merge into the background, drawing your attention to the punctuation marks of the eyes, mouth and nostrils. However, the vibrant, geometric shapes are overlaid in such a way as to suggest and complete the form of the head.

CHEETAHS
Judy Wood

The fur of these two cheetahs almost merges, differentiated only by the flow of the spots and the subtle grouting. The large pieces of tile used to create the rocks on which the animals are sitting create a strong base and add solidity to the picture. The harvest moon provides a light background to frame and illuminate the cats.

WHITE STAG
Judy Wood

Here the large tiles create the sinuousness of the stag's body and contrast with the busy, crackle-effect background that suggests movement of, perhaps, a snowstorm. The surrounding frame cleverly echoes the pattern and colours of the stag's saddle and harness.

ROMEO
Mary Taylor

In this mosaic, the tiles follow the direction of the cockerel's plumage, which stands out against the regularity of the blue background. Interest has been added to the frame by introducing some variety into the tone and tint of the tiles.

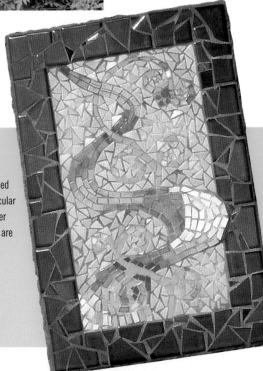

TUSCAN RIBBON
Laura Aiken

Rich colours and the large tile fragments used in the frame give this design a strong, muscular feel. The curve of the ribbon has been further emphasized by building up the tiles so they are raised above the background.

KNIGHT IN ARMOR
Judy Wood

Another piece in which pictorial elements are given different treatments. The anatomical plates of the horse give it a graceful power and establish the foreground of the picture, in contrast to the small square tiles used in the sky and the rectangles that so effectively create the walled town in the background.

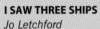

I SAW THREE SHIPS
Jo Letchford

Here, three old-fashioned ships under full sail have been mosaiced in intricate detail. The varying shades of brown used on the wooden hulls add interest, while the mixed blues of the background allow sea and sky to merge into one.

LUCERNE
Jo Letchford

This picture is strengthened by the simplicity with which the tiles are laid out – each element is tiled in strong and unwavering horizontal bands, which build the solidity of the scene as a whole.

PATTERNED GALLEON
Jo Letchford

The solid and graceful shape of the boat's hull and the precise, flat background hold this piece together, stopping the vibrant, almost discordant patterns of the sails from fragmenting the picture. A subtle colour palette lends the piece an overall softness.

COLOURFUL WORLD
Jeanine Gerlofsma

The carefree design and delicacy of colour in this picture give a joyous, child-like quality to the finished piece. The way colours are picked up in the different figures and areas of the design cleverly weave the elements together to give a unifying effect that clearly underlines the message of the image itself.

PAISLEY PATTERN
Marcelo José de Melo

The hexagonal shape and darker framing tiles strengthen the central composition of a paisley motif, transformed into a cornucopia of flowers with a rich sense of abundance.

FLORA
Irina Charny

This beautiful mosaic composition bursts with life and vitality and is rich in ideas and design. The entire area of the figure is occupied with a huge variety of flower motifs that cleverly balance and complement one another.

NATIVE AMERICAN CHIEF
Dino Semilia

This portrait uses a palette of traditional Native American colours to provide the tonal range for this naturalistic picture. Cropping the head fills the frame and strengthens the composition.

YOUNG PROFESSOR
Marcelo José de Melo

A simple, contrasting palette and bold outline create an effective and strong portrait, whilst the contrasting noise of the patterns of the background and the shirt add a decorative dimension and charm.

LADY IN SATIN
Paula Macleod

This is a highly skilled piece in which a mixture of materials (smalti, unglazed porcelain, satin and found objects) have been combined with meticulous care to create the soft tones of the subject's skin and the strong light and shadow.

BALLERINA
Irina Charny

An inner frame seems to be trying to confine the angular limbs of the ballerina which are elongated to fill the picture. The cloth she holds has a billowing fullness, which contrasts well with the spiky feel of the figure. The colours of the frame echo the palette of the main picture.

DIONYSUS
Rosalind Wates

A piece in the classical mosaic tradition depicting the god of wine and fertility (known as Bacchus to the Romans). The circular frame echoes and draws the eye to the shape of the pitcher at the heart of the composition.

MATERIALS
AND
TOOLS

This chapter contains information on the variety of materials you can use in mosaic work, plus explanations of the tools you will need. You will see that there are very few specialist materials, as many everyday household items can be used when creating mosaics.

WORKSPACE

If you have some spare space within your home, you can have the luxury of setting up a dedicated workspace for your mosaic work. If space is at a premium, then you can convert an old tray into a 'workshop' on which to keep your work-in-progress and your essential tools, working on a kitchen or dining table when you have the opportunity. Either way, the requirements of the workspace are the same.

Light

The most important thing is a good source of light so that you can see what you are doing and work without straining your eyes. Ideally, this should be daylight, as different types of electric bulbs can distort the colours of your tiles and the finished piece may look completely different when displayed in natural light.

An anglepoise lamp is always useful to augment natural light, or to use when you are working on very close-up, detailed work where your own shadow will block out other sources of light.

Ventilation

The workspace should also be well ventilated. Parts of the mosaic process, such as cutting baseboards or mixing grout, produce dust and, wherever possible, these jobs are better undertaken out of doors.

Worksurface

A solid, stable worktop is another essential, particularly when you are breaking tiles. A kitchen table is fine, provided it is sturdy and doesn't wobble. The worktop should be at a good height in relation to the chair or stool you sit on to avoid straining your back. (It is good practice to get into the habit of taking a break at least every quarter of an hour, to straighten your back, and to stretch out your arms and shoulders.)

It is best to keep a part of the worktop separate for working on drawings and designs. The area you use for tiling will get grout, glue and other materials on it, which will inevitably contaminate every clean piece of paper you bring near it.

Water

You will also need access to a sink or running water, particularly when cleaning the grout from the tiles. Be careful about tipping grout down domestic sinks in particular, as you risk permanently blocking the waste pipes. Always dispose of grout from any process by scraping as much of it as possible into a rubbish bag or dustbin. Try to minimize the amount you wash down the sink. Again, it is better if you have access to an outside area with a tap for cleaning purposes.

Flooring

A very important consideration is the floor or floor covering you work on. You need something hard, on which you can easily spot and sweep up the shards and splinters of tiles. Carpets will quickly be ruined if exposed to the by-products of mosaic. If you have no choice, then buy some heavy-duty polythene or a plastic tarpaulin to protect carpets whilst you are working.

Storage

The other important thing you need is storage for the variety of tiles, grouts and tools you will be using. A set of strong, deep shelves or an old cabinet is ideal. Ask friends and families to save old jars and containers for you to keep all your tiles in.

TYPES OF TILES

The mosaic pieces featured in this book have been made with two types of tile – glass tesserae and ordinary household wall tiles.

Tesserae

Tesserae is the Latin word originally used to describe mosaic pieces and these are the tiles most people now associate with mosaics. They are used extensively in architectural mosaics on buildings and in public spaces, as well as in swimming pools. These tiles are made from coloured glass and come in a huge range of hues and finishes, including metallic colours.

▲ Glass tesserae are available in a huge range of bright, solid colours.

These tiles usually measure about 25mm (1 inch) square. The top surface is completely smooth; underneath, the edges are bevelled and the bottom surface roughened to aid adhesion to glues and grouts. Sometimes you will see these tiles sold in sheet form, where the tiles are neatly pre-spaced and held together on a mounting sheet, or by a net on the back, so that they can be quickly applied to cover

◀ Just looking at the colours and textures of the tiles can provide wonderful inspiration for your mosaic work.

large, flat areas. You can buy them like this and detach them from their mounting sheet, but, as you will probably want a variety of tiles to follow the designs in this book, you will find it better to buy the tiles loose or in mixed batches from specialist suppliers.

Glass tesserae

Glass tesserae, not surprisingly, have all the characteristics of glass – they are very resilient and hardwearing, and when you cut and work with them, they will often break in an unpredictable way. They also have a tendency to leave sharp edges – small nicks and cuts on your fingers are the inevitable consequence of working with these tiles. Their density makes them ideal for use out of doors, providing the glues, grouts and baseboards you combine them with have the same weather-proofness (see pages 39 and 43).

▲ *Using a variety of subtly different shades and tones in a background can prevent it looking flat.*

Their best feature, however, must be the richness of colour they offer the mosaicist – you can produce breathtaking results following even the simplest design through the careful choice and combination of these tiles.

▼ *Many tesserae tiles have beautiful shading embedded in them, giving an attractive striped or marble effect.*

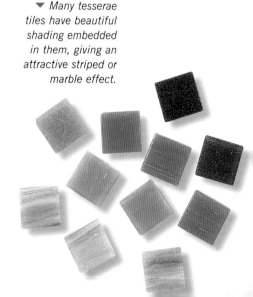

▲ *Monochrome colours can be just as striking as vibrantly coloured tiles – see the Charlie Chaplin mosaic on page 218.*

Household tiles

Household tiles – the type used on walls, rather than floors as the latter are thicker and heavier to work with – offer different possibilities. These tiles come in a range of sizes, most commonly 10cm (4 inches) square. Generally they have a smooth glazed surface, below which is a ceramic base.

These also come in a variety of colours, patterns and designs, although the colours tend to be more muted than the glass tesserae. Some people find ceramic tiles easier to work with – you can nibble the tiles more easily with tile nippers (see pages 53–54). You can also create designs with larger component pieces (see the designs on pages 206–209), whilst recycling old tiles, or using patterned tiles, also offers some interesting effects. The drawback with these tiles is that they tend to be less hard-wearing and, if used for outdoor mosaics, are liable to be shattered by frost.

▼ *The larger size of these tiles can be useful when creating mosaics where the design demands large, unbroken areas of colour.*

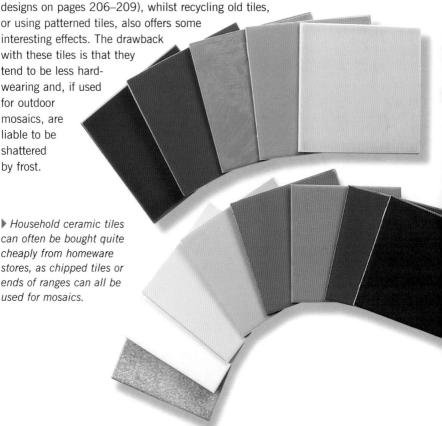

▶ *Household ceramic tiles can often be bought quite cheaply from homeware stores, as chipped tiles or ends of ranges can all be used for mosaics.*

Other materials

There are countless other materials you can use for mosaic that are not covered in this book – traditional stone and marble for example. In fact, you can create mosaics with just about any material that lends itself to being positioned and glued to a base – seashells, buttons, eggshells, broken plates, broken flowerpots and garden pebbles can all produce wonderful results.

You can also combine other materials with your mosaics. In this book you will see examples of diamanté, glitter, dolls' eyes and other 'found objects' being incorporated into the finished design. In the end, the choice of materials is down to you. You can work with traditional materials and techniques, or experiment with almost anything that gives a result that you find pleasing.

▲ *Buttons are useful for adding detail to clothing, as in the Rag Doll on page 184.*

▲ *Square mirror tiles can be used alongside ceramic or glass tesserae.*

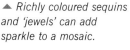
▲ *Richly coloured sequins and 'jewels' can add sparkle to a mosaic.*

▶ *Seashells can either be used in a mosaic or to create a frame around a tiled design.*

EQUIPMENT

Don't be overwhelmed by the array of tools and equipment shown on these pages. When you look closely, you will see that you probably already have many of the pieces stored either in a toolbox or in a stationery drawer.

In addition to the tools shown here, you will need a supply of old rags for polishing and cleaning and newspapers for grouting on. A dustpan and brush is also best kept close at hand so you can clean up as you go.

Drawing materials
1 Plain paper for drawing
Graph paper for scaling drawings
Tracing paper to transfer the drawing to the baseboard
2 A range of both hard and soft pencils
3 Pens for outlining designs
4 A clear ruler for marking out grids

Baseboards
5 MDF or other baseboard (see pages 38–39)
6 PVA glue to water down and use as a primer
7 Household paintbrush to apply primer

Tile-cutting tools
8 Tile nippers for splitting and shaping small pieces and for nibbling curves and shapes (see pages 53–54)
9 Tile scorer for use on household tiles – use with a steel rule or straight edge to scribe straight lines in the surface glaze, then use the tile snappers to snap the tile along this line (see page 53)

10 **11** **12** **13**

14

15

Glue
10 PVA wood glue (see page 57)

11 Small paintbrush to stick the tiles to the baseboard

Grout
12 Disposable container for mixing grout

13 Water and acrylic paint/pigment for mixing with grout

14 Ready-mix grout and grout powder to which you add water

15 Small squeegee for applying grout

16 Sponge for removing excess grout

16

Protective gear
17 Goggles – vital, particularly when working with nippers and glass tiles that are prone to shatter unexpectedly

18 Rubber gloves, for working with grout

19 Face mask, to use with any power tools, such as drills or saws

18

17

19

SURFACES, GLUES AND GROUTS

The choice of material you use to glue your mosaics to, and the glue you use, is almost as important as the choice of tiles. With the right glues, mosaics tiles can be persuaded to stick to almost anything – you will see mosaics applied to an astonishing range of three-dimensional objects including vases, bottles and items of furniture.

Most of the pieces in this book, however, have been produced using medium density fibreboard (MDF) as the baseboard material, to which tiles have been stuck using PVA glue.

▼ *Use mosaics to embellish all manner of household items, from flowerpots to wooden picture frames and storage boxes.*

Medium density fibreboard (MDF)

MDF is a man-made material created from fine wood fibres glued together under heat and pressure. MDF has been used for a number of years to make wall cabinets, shelving and kitchen units, and is available in different thicknesses and sizes, up to 2.4 x 1.2m (8 x 4 feet).

MDF has a number of advantages over materials like plywood or hardboard. It is a very stable material, which, providing it is kept dry, is unlikely to warp. The surface is completely even and smooth without any grain and readily accepts glue. MDF can also be drilled and sawn fairly easily so quite complex shapes can be cut using a jigsaw or router. Care needs to be taken when sawing or machining this material – the dust produced can be an irritant so you should always work in a ventilated area and wear a face mask.

As mentioned, MDF does not like moisture, and pieces that become wet will swell and buckle, causing tiles to detach. It is, therefore, definitely not suitable for pieces that will be outside, or in areas of moisture (such as bath or shower rooms). In these situations, use marine plywood (see below).

Marine plywood

An alternative to MDF is marine plywood, which was specifically developed for use in boat construction and is resistant to water. This is better suited for outdoor use. However, care still needs to be taken when using this for mosaics, not only by using suitable tiles, grouts and glues that are water- and frost-resistant, but also ensuring that any exposed surfaces of the plywood are treated with several generous coats of weatherproof paint or varnish.

GLUES

Choosing the right glue is just as important a part of creating a mosaic as choosing which tiles to use.

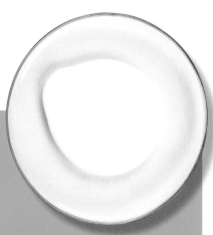

PVA glue

For sticking most tiles to MDF or other wooden baseboards, you will find a PVA wood glue is the most practical adhesive. These glues are white in colour until they set, when they dry clear. This has the advantage that you are able to see the glue on the board whilst you are working with it, but that any glue that finds its way on to the surface of the tiles will not be so noticeable once it has dried. These glues dry relatively quickly (in a few hours) but not so quickly that you feel under pressure whilst working on a piece.

▲ *You may find it easier to decant some glue on to a saucer, rather than dipping the brush directly into the glue pot.*

◀ *PVA glue can be purchased in craft shops and homeware and DIY stores.*

Applying glue

When applying glue, it is very important only to put as much down as you can work with in a reasonable time. It is always best to have practised laying the pieces on the board first before putting down any glue in order to check that the design fits together. You will get into a real mess if you start retrieving glued pieces from the baseboard to try and re-cut them.

Specialist glues

For other applications you can use specialist glues. For outdoor work you may want to use epoxy adhesives. These have better weather resistance and dry like a hard resin. *two-part epoxy resin*

They are, however, more difficult to work with. These glues have two components, supplied in separate tubes or containers, which you have to mix together in equal amounts. They also have to be mixed thoroughly to ensure the components react properly with each other. The glue dries more quickly than PVA so you have to work with smaller batches. You will also find epoxy adhesives messier to work with and harder to clean from your hands and tools.

You will find a range of glues available at DIY stores that will allow you to stick different materials together, including glass and ceramics. Some glues, however, can be discounted as unsuitable for mosaics. So-called 'super glues' that dry in a matter of seconds do not give you sufficient working time for mosaic applications. Always remember to read the instructions carefully and follow the health and safety guidelines.

Apply the glue with a spatula or a brush to the baseboard. Don't apply too thick a layer. Use just enough to adhere the back of the tile to the baseboard – you do not want the pieces 'floating' in glue. For detailed areas using small tiles, you may wish to apply a dab of glue to the back of the tile with a fine brush.

Don't worry too much about residue of glue between the tiles – this will be concealed later when you grout the piece. Do try to avoid getting glue on the surface of the mosaics as this will only add work when you come to the final clean-up.

If you do get into a mess, you can wipe off PVA glue with a damp cloth before it sets. Once set, however, the glue has a plastic, impervious feel and cannot be removed by a damp cloth, however hard you rub.

dark grout

grey grout

white grout

GROUT

Grouting is the final act that really transforms your mosaic piece. The grout holds the pieces of the design together, not only literally, but visually as well. As you wash off the excess grout you will find that your design will have a new completeness and 'togetherness' that can be quite breathtaking.

grout powder

For mosaic pictures that are not subject to wear or weather, it is normally sufficient to use a ready-mix grout/adhesive of the type used on wall tiles around the home. This type of grout is widely available, inexpensive and fairly easy to work with.

Coloured grout

You need to give consideration to the colour of the grout for each particular piece. Ready-mix grouts are usually white and this is seldom the best colour to use on a mosaic design as it can fragment the picture, particularly where the gaps between tiles are large.

It is therefore best to tone down the grout by adding colour to it. Use acrylic or other water-based paints and add these a little at a time to the grout. Mix the grout in a separate, re-sealable container, such as an old ice-cream carton, to ensure you have sufficient grout for the whole area. The last thing you want is to run out of coloured grout halfway through and then have the problem of trying to mix and match a second batch to complete the piece.

For most mosaics, a mid-grey is the safest colour choice. This will tend to enhance the colours of the tiles it surrounds, rather than clash or overpower them. This is particularly true for pictures in which there is a varied colour palette of

Heavy-duty grout

If you are grouting pieces that are going to be outside or on floor areas where they will be subject to wear, it is better to use cement-based grouts which are harder wearing and waterproof. These come as a powder to which you add water and mix. It takes practice to get the consistency right and your options for adding colour are restricted. These grouts are usually grey and do not take colour well. Coloured cement grouts are available from specialist suppliers, but are more expensive and the choice of colours is limited.

heavy-duty grout

lights and darks. You can add further colours to the grey – such as reds or blues – or experiment with purer mid-tones of colours to complement the colour palette of a particular piece. Compare the mosaics shown on the left and right sides of this page to see the effect the colour of the grout has on the overall appearance of the piece.

For more abstract pieces, or ones with limited colours, experiment with heavier coloured grout and even use a colour that clashes with the tile colours. The darker colours will tend to enhance the tiles, making them more vibrant, but will also produce a 'net effect' over the design. Very bright coloured grouts will have a tendency to 'zing' against the tiles in a way that can distract from the design. It is wise to experiment with such effects on small test pieces before adding heavily coloured grouts with irreversible results.

The white pigment in ordinary grout means that you can only make pastel shades when you add paints or pigments, not pure, primary colours. If you want to try strong colours, you will need to obtain pre-coloured ready-mix grouts.

white grout

mid-grey grout

red grout

blue grout

TECHNIQUES

Once you've mastered the basic techniques
featured in this chapter, you will be able to
make any of the mosaics in the Directory
section starting on page 76, or create your
own designs.

▶ *Clashing colours can work well together, as with this bunch of vibrantly coloured artificial tulips.*

GETTING IDEAS

There are many sources that can provide you with ideas for new and interesting mosaic designs, and your starting point should be to look at a whole range of visual sources, not just mosaics. Fabrics, gift wrap, wallpaper, greetings cards and food packaging can all provide ideas or suggest shapes and colour combinations that are visually strong but which you may not have previously considered.

Ideally, you should keep a scrapbook or file in which to store pictures, illustrations, samples, or colour swatches that you come across. Collect and squirrel away anything that grabs your attention, even if, at the time, you are not quite sure why you like it. Charity

▲ *Greetings cards are a great source of inspiration, often containing small details or patterns ideal for mosaic work.*

◀ *This brightly coloured soft toy provided the starting point for the angel fish designs featured on pages 166–167.*

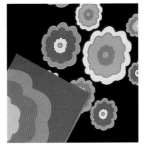

◀ *Fabrics and gift wrap often include simple floral motifs, which can be recreated in mosaic.*

shops and flea markets can be a great source of ideas, where you can find illustrations in old books, old postcards and motifs from fabrics.

Often, an illustration from a book or magazine will be too complex to attempt in mosaic. Look and see how you could simplify the design, or try to isolate just one part of the design that you could enlarge and use on its own as an abstract image.

Children's drawings often have a freshness and simplicity on which you can base a mosaic design, or, if you look around your own home, you may find old pictures and heirlooms that provoke special memories. In fact, the mosaic of the young girl featured on page 243 was inspired by a picture painted by the author's father, which hung in her bedroom as a child.

▲ *Design reference books can be a great source of inspiration, such as these books featuring carpet and tile designs.*

▶ *These fabric swatches are taken from cotton head scarves featuring strong patterns which can be traced over.*

WORKING WITH COLOUR

One of the most useful tools in your work is the colour wheel. This is a 'map' of the way colours work and react with each other. Colour wheels are used as a guide by many people who rely on using colour in their work, including interior designers, painters, graphic artists, fashion designers and even gardeners.

    The colour wheels produced by a painter, carefully mixing each combination of pigments, move smoothly through the whole spectrum of colours without any noticeable jumps. As a mosaicist you are limited by the colours of tiles that are available or that you can easily obtain, but the basic 'rules' of colour still apply.

How the colour wheel works

Spaced equally around the wheel are the three primary colours – red, blue and yellow. These are the pure colours that cannot be mixed from any other colours. In between, and equidistant from, each primary is the secondary colour you obtain when you mix equal amounts of the two primaries – orange between the red and yellow, purple between red and blue, green between blue and yellow.

Between the primary and secondary colours are the results of combining primaries in different amounts. So, as you move from orange to red, you get a

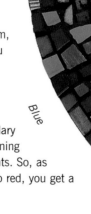

Red

Purple

Blue

▶ *The colour wheel is an important tool for all artists, demonstrating the relationships between the three primary colours.*

progressively deeper orange; as you move away from green to yellow, you get progressively lighter greens, and so on. The closer you get to the blue part of the wheel, the cooler the colours are – blues, greens and purples. As you move the other way toward the red zone of the wheel, the colours are warmer. The wheel is an important guide to the mood colours will create. Cooler colours are generally used to produce a more soothing effect; the hot colours give energy and impact (which may not be so easy to live with in a decorative piece).

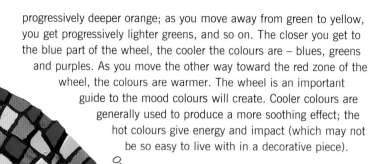

Orange

Yellow

Green

cool colours

ADVANCE AND RECEDE

Warm colours tend to advance to the front of the picture and the cool ones to recede. Use this knowledge in your mosaic picture making.

blues recede

warm colours

reds advance

Complementary colours

The wheel also shows you which colours
contrast with each other. The so-called
complementary colours are those that are found
opposite each other on the wheel – blue and
orange, red and green, yellow and purple. Using
a background that is complementary to the
main image will enhance and intensify the
foreground colour of the design. If you use
complementary colours of exactly the same
tone, the effect is even more intense as the
two colours will shimmer against
each other – an effect
which can be distracting
and should therefore be
used with caution.

◀ *Using the colour
wheel will help
you to understand
how colours
relate, and which
bring out the best
in each other.*

◀ *When using
fabric as the
inspiration for
your design, you
can either match
the colourways in
the original, or
create your own
colour scheme.*

Using colour

The trick with colour is to play with all sorts of combinations before committing anything to the mosaic baseboard with glue. Refer to the colour wheel to give you ideas. Play with clusters of different coloured tiles and see what effects can be created by using a different 'temperature' of palette or by introducing colour opposites to create an accent within the motif you are working on. In this book you will see a number of examples where a completely different end result has been achieved from the same source drawing simply by choosing a different colour palette (see, for example, the dinosaur motif on pages 182–183).

▲ *These two dinosaurs use the same template (see page 182), but the colours give different results.*

Don't forget that just as important as the choice of tiles is the choice of colour you choose for the grout. In fact, the grout has a colour and tone that will surround and react with every tile in your design, so it may be the most important colour decision you make (see examples on pages 42–43). So, consider the grout colour from the beginning and refer to the colour wheel when considering your choice.

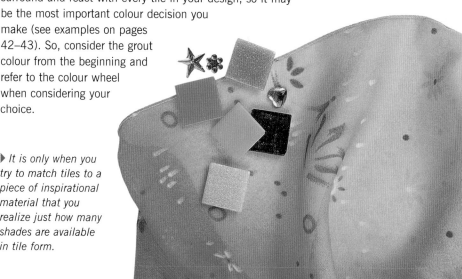

▶ *It is only when you try to match tiles to a piece of inspirational material that you realize just how many shades are available in tile form.*

SCALING A DRAWING

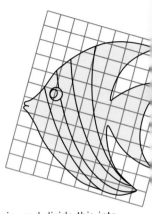

To enlarge a drawing to the size required for the finished mosaic you can use the grid technique.

If using the designs from this book, you will see that they already have a grid drawn over them. If using a design from another source, either draw a grid of squares over the original, or draw a grid onto a transparent material, such as tracing paper, that you can place over the original to avoid damaging it.

Next, take a sheet of paper the size of the finished mosaic, and divide this into the same number of squares as cover the original design. Alternatively, decide how many times larger you want the design to be – for example, five times larger – then draw the full-size grid with squares that are larger by exactly this factor (in the example, five times the size). You might find it helpful to number or colour code both grids identically down the side and along the top.

1 ▶ Draw the full size grid in pencil using a clear plastic ruler so that you can see the lines more easily.

2 ▲ Draw the horizontal lines. Now look carefully at the original design and see where each of the main lines in the design crosses the grid. Go to the same square on the full-size drawing and put a dot in the same place on the grid. Follow the lines of the original drawing, placing a dot on your enlarged drawing at every point they cross the grid.

3 ▼ Join all the dots to recreate the lines of the original. Sometimes a key point in the design will be hanging in the middle of a square. Use a straight edge to see exactly how far the point is below the nearest horizontal line, then how far it is to the left or right of the nearest horizontal. Create these lines on the enlarged grid to position the point accurately within the drawing at their intersection.

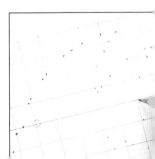

CUTTING TILES

Being able to cut tiles with precision is something that only comes with practice, but provided you have the right tools and sufficient patience, anyone can master this skill.

Cutting tesserae

Glass tesserae are brittle and, because of their small size, the only way to cut them is using tile nippers, but there is a skill to this. You cut the tile by a mixture of the pressure of the grip of the nippers combined with a slight snapping, downward action. If you try to break a glass tesserae just by the pressure of the nippers alone, it will most likely shatter.

The other technique with glass tesserae is to use the tile nippers to nibble away at the tile a small piece at a time, for example to cut out circles.

Cutting household tiles

If you are working with household tiles you can use a variety of tools, as shown in the steps below and on page 54.

1 ▲ Use a metal straight edge and a scribe to score the glazed surface at intervals along the width of the tile.

2 ▼ Use the tile snapper to break the tile cleanly along each score line.

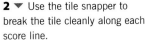

3 ◀ You now have a number of strips of tile of equal widths.

4 ▶ Using the tile nippers, snap each strip into square tiles of the same size (with practice you will be able to do this 'by eye', but at first you may want to measure each square, marking where you are to cut with a chinagraph crayon).

5 ▶ Circles and curves can be cut using the tile nippers to nibble away small sections of tile. Draw the shape you want to achieve on to the tile first, using a chinagraph crayon.

7 ▼ To create a series of tiles to lay in a curve, divide the strips as flat-bottomed triangles or wedges. Experiment with the angles of the sides, making the wedges more pointed for tight curves, or squarer for longer, gentler curves.

6 ▶ Triangles can be created by cutting the strips of tile at the required angles.

MAKING A MOSAIC

All the mosaics in this book are made using what is known as the 'direct method' of mosaic. The tiles are glued directly to a baseboard and then, when set, the piece is grouted and finished. It is by far the simplest way to produce mosaics, and avoids having to master any difficult transfer techniques.

This sequence of step-by-step photographs and instructions shows how to make the beach hut featured on pages 240–241, but you can use this method for any mosaic.

Creating the design

1 ▶ Start from a clear outline drawing of the design. If you are working from a design in this book, follow the instructions on page 52 for scaling the drawing. If you are creating your own design from scratch, or following a motif from another source, it is advisable to work in pencil so that you can make changes easily. The drawing should be the actual size of the piece, and when finished, the drawing should look simple, or even empty. If you put in too much detail this will not work in mosaic. Keep the design uncluttered and open – the tiles will do the work for you later.

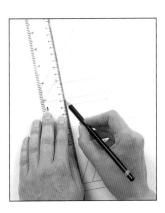

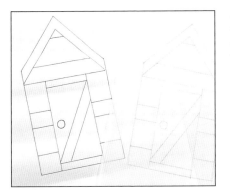

2 ◀ When you are happy with your finished drawing, copy it on to tracing paper. Tape the drawing to a table or worktop, then tape the tracing paper over this so that it does not move. Carefully trace over the drawing using a hard pencil.

3 ▶ When you have traced the drawing, turn it over, re-tape it to your worktop, and then carefully trace over the back of the design, this time using a very soft pencil. The idea is that this pencil line on the back of the drawing will act like carbon paper and transfer to the baseboard when you go over the drawing the right way round (in step 5).

4 ▼ Cut your baseboard to the right shape and size. It is best to do this now, rather than when the mosaic is finished, as you risk damaging the design. Prime the baseboard using some watered-down PVA adhesive, applied with a small household paintbrush. Allow the board to dry.

5 ▶ Position your tracing the right way round over the baseboard. Once again, it is wise to tape the tracing paper in position. Carefully go over the drawing with a hard pencil, pressing firmly, so that the pencil line on the back of the drawing transfers to the baseboard. When you have gone over the entire drawing, remove the tracing paper and go over any faint or missing areas.

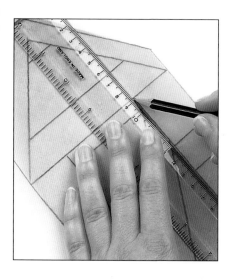

Adding the tiles

6 ▶ Start cutting your tiles to size (see pages 53–54). Work on areas of the same colour and lay the tiles on to the baseboard without any glue to check that they fit.

7 ▶ Take extra care with 'feature' tiles (like the circular door handle in this example). Be prepared to have several attempts at a difficult cut before you get it right. It's far better to discard a few tiles than to have an unsatisfactory end result because of one poorly cut tile.

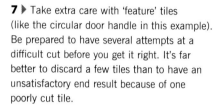

8 ◀ When you have an area of the design completed, you can begin gluing pieces to the baseboard. Use a small brush to dab an even amount of glue on to the back of each tile. Take care not to get glue on to the surface of the tile. Place the tiles, leaving a small gap of about 2mm (⅛ inch) around them, to allow the grout to penetrate later.

9 ◀ Take care to cut the tiles equally, particularly in the case of a symmetrical design like this example. Where there are bands of tiles of one colour and thickness, work on these together, comparing the size of each cut tile with the others in the group and making any adjustments with the tile nippers before gluing them down.

10 ▶ Add the small and difficult filler tiles at the end. It is easier to drop these into a gap between tiles, than to try to position them correctly on the bare baseboard at the beginning.

11 ▼ Check the finished piece for any odd-looking tiles or wobbly lines. If necessary, you can prise out a tile with an old screwdriver before the glue has set completely. Once the glue has dried, however, this is almost impossible to do without splintering the tile you are trying to remove and probably damaging those surrounding it. Leave the glue to set for at least a day before grouting the piece.

Grouting the mosaic

12 ▶ Before starting to grout for the first time, read the notes on grout and colour (see pages 42–43) as in most cases it is best to use a grey or coloured grout. If you are colouring the grout yourself, begin by adding the paint or pigment to the mixing bowl first.

13 ◀ Add the grout to the bowl. The grout shown here is ready mixed; if you are mixing your own, make this up first in a separate container, following the manufacturer's instructions. Remember to make sufficient grout to cover the entire piece as it will be hard to match the colour of the grout in a second mix. Make sure you mix it really well so that the colour is uniform.

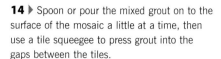

14 ▶ Spoon or pour the mixed grout on to the surface of the mosaic a little at a time, then use a tile squeegee to press grout into the gaps between the tiles.

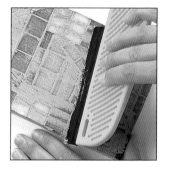

15 ▲ Spread the grout repeatedly over the surface, then press it down again to ensure the gaps are properly filled. Use the squeegee to wipe the excess away.

▶ The finished mosaic. Other colourways are featured on pages 240–241.

16 ▲ Wipe over the mosaic with a damp sponge to reveal the surface of the tiles. Don't over-wet the sponge or you will disturb the grout between the tiles. Leave for about half an hour, then, before the grout is completely hard, polish and clean off any remaining residue from the tile surface with a soft, dry cloth.

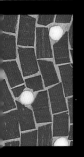

PATTERN SELECTOR

The following pages provide an at-a-glance guide to all the designs contained in the Directory, which begins on page 77. Flick through the pages and see which mosaics catch your eye. You can then either recreate them exactly as they are featured here, or change the colourway and make them into something truly individual.

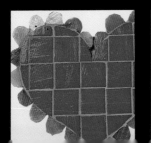

**PATTERNS
AND
BORDERS**

PAGE 76

PAGE 77

PAGE 78

PAGE 79

PAGE 79

PAGE 80

PAGE 81

PAGE 82

PAGE 83

PAGE 84

PAGE 85

PAGE 85

PAGE 86

PAGE 86

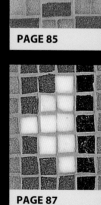

PAGE 87

PAGE 88

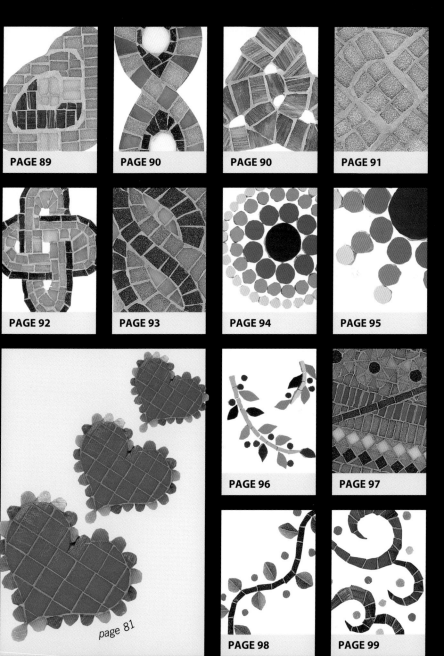

PAGE 89

PAGE 90

PAGE 90

PAGE 91

PAGE 92

PAGE 93

PAGE 94

PAGE 95

page 81

PAGE 96

PAGE 97

PAGE 98

PAGE 99

SYMBOLS

PAGE 100

PAGE 101

PAGE 102

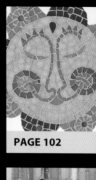

PAGE 103

PAGE 104

PAGE 105

PAGE 106

PAGE 107

PAGE 108

PAGE 109

PAGE 110

PAGE 111

PAGE 112

PAGE 113

PAGE 114

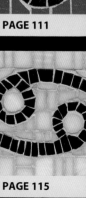

PAGE 115

PATTERN SELECTOR

LETTERS
AND
NUMBERS

PAGE 116

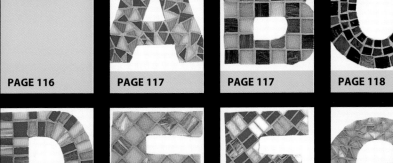

PAGE 117

PAGE 117

PAGE 118

PAGE 118

PAGE 119

PAGE 119

PAGE 120

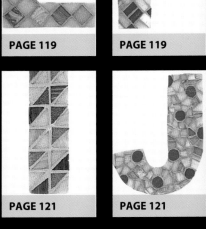
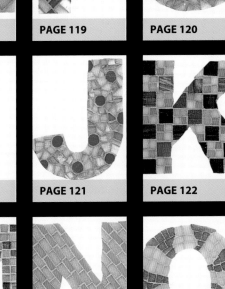

PAGE 120

PAGE 121

PAGE 121

PAGE 122

PAGE 122

PAGE 123

PAGE 123

PAGE 124

PAGE 124

PAGE 125

PAGE 125

PAGE 126

PAGE 126

PAGE 127

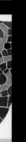

PAGE 127

PAGE 128

page 126

PAGE 128

PAGE 129

PAGE 129

PAGE 130

PAGE 131

PAGE 131

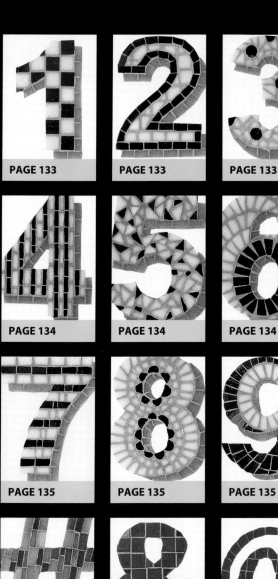

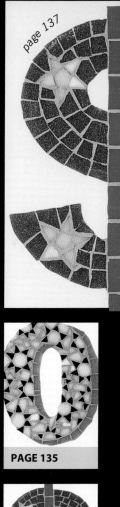

page 137

PAGE 133

PAGE 133

PAGE 133

PAGE 134

PAGE 134

PAGE 134

PAGE 135

PAGE 135

PAGE 135

PAGE 135

PAGE 136

PAGE 136

PAGE 137

PAGE 137

PATTERN SELECTOR

ANIMALS AND
BIRDS

PAGE 138

PAGE 139

PAGE 140

PAGE 141

PAGE 142

PAGE 143

PAGE 144

PAGE 145

PAGE 146

PAGE 147

PAGE 148

PAGE 149

PAGE 150

PAGE 151

PAGES 152–153

PAGE 154

PAGE 155

PAGE 156

PAGE 157

PAGE 158

PAGE 159

PAGE 160

PAGE 161

PAGES 162–163

**MARINE
LIFE**

PAGE 164

PAGE 165

PAGES 166–167

PAGE 168

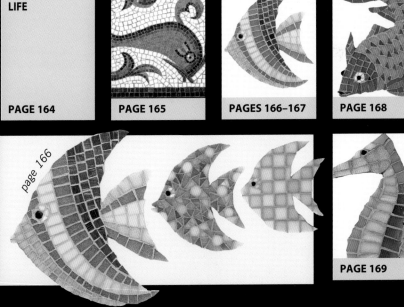

page 166

PAGE 169

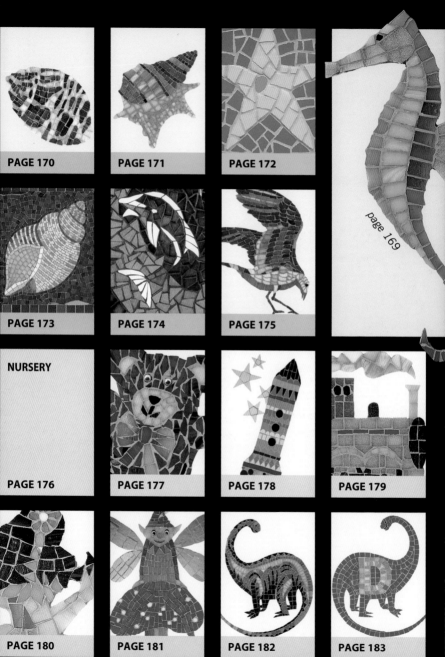

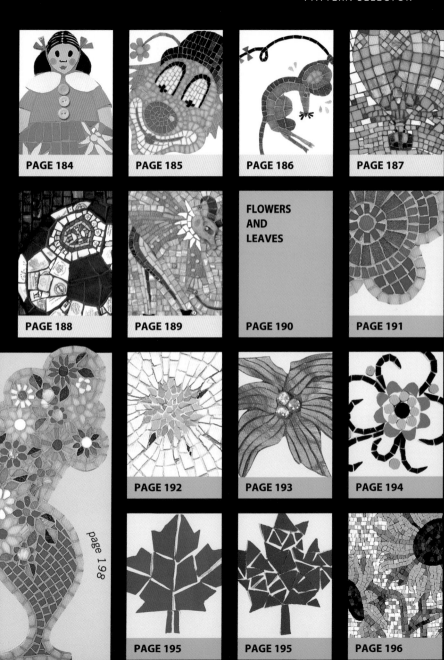

PAGE 184

PAGE 185

PAGE 186

PAGE 187

PAGE 188

PAGE 189

**FLOWERS
AND
LEAVES**

PAGE 190

PAGE 191

page 198

PAGE 192

PAGE 193

PAGE 194

PAGE 195

PAGE 195

PAGE 196

PAGE 197

PAGE 198

PAGE 199

PAGE 199

PAGE 200

PAGE 201

PAGE 202

PAGE 202

pages 204–205

PAGE 203

PAGES 204–205

PAGE 206

PAGE 207

PAGE 208

PAGE 209

FIGURES

PAGE 210

PAGE 211

PAGE 212

PAGE 213

PAGE 214

PAGE 215

PAGE 216

PAGE 217

PAGE 218

PAGE 219

PAGE 220

PAGE 221

PAGE 222

PAGE 223

PAGE 224

PAGE 225

STILL LIFE

PAGE 226

PAGE 227

PAGE 228

PAGE 229

PAGE 230

PAGE 231

PAGE 232

PAGE 233

page 227

PAGE 234

PAGE 235

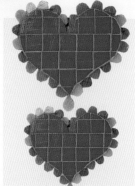

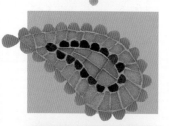

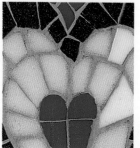

PATTERNS AND BORDERS

Patterns and borders provide a good starting point for the mosaicist to develop his or her skills and gain an understanding of the possibilities of working in this medium. Many of the patterns in this chapter use the simplest of designs – in some cases without even the need to cut any tiles – yet the variations that are possible through choice of colour or simple changes in the positioning or repetition of the design are infinite. The patterns can be used as decorative surrounds to other pictorial designs, or used in the traditional manner as decoration on walls or floors in their own right.

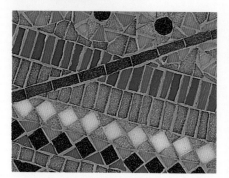

CHILDREN IN A CIRCLE

Each figure in this circle is an adaptation of the same motif. Placed in a circle the figures become a frame for a picture, mirror or clock. This is an ideal design for using up offcuts of tiles.

COLOUR PALETTE
All and everything

scale drawing

As an alternative to using the figures in a circle, the elements of the design could be positioned in a conventional, linear frieze.

For a different look, try surrounding the figures with a dark background (such as an ultramarine blue) to hold them together and strengthen the paper-chain effect.

SPIRAL PATTERNS

The main trick to these pieces is to draw a perfect sprial.
Once you have achieved that, you can simply fill in the line
of the spiral (cutting the tiles at an angle to join them in a
flowing way), then decorate the spiral with circles, dots, leaves,
flowers or other motifs of your choice.

*Work outwards from the
centre, first tiling the
backbone of the spiral,
then positioning the cogs
and circles.*

MIX & MATCH

This motif can be used
to provide a firework
background to the space
rocket on page 178.

scale drawing

COLOUR PALETTE

scale drawing

COLOUR PALETTE

Again, work from the centre with these more organic versions of the spiral shown on the left. Experiment with increasing the size of the leaves and fruit slightly as you move outwards, to increase the sense of growth.

scale drawing

COLOUR PALETTE

HEARTS

The heart is an essential motif which can be adapted in a variety of ways. Here it is drawn with very different proportions – on this page thin and sinuous, on the facing page fuller and fatter. The two examples have also been filled using different techniques – on this page following the outline of the shape, on the facing page using a flat fill.

COLOUR PALETTE

To create these clover leaves, first draw a cross as the axis on which to place each repeat of the design. You could also experiment with a repeat of six or eight hearts in a circle. Use a protractor to get the correct angles between the arms of the design (60° for a repeat of six hearts; 45° for a repeat of eight hearts).

scale drawing

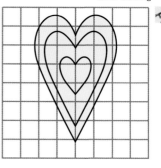

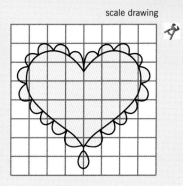

scale drawing

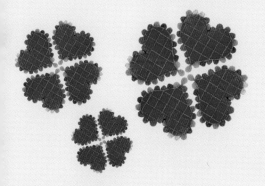

To give symmetry to the flat fill in this version of the heart, start working from the centre, laying out all the whole tiles, then cut the individual tiles to fill up the space to the edge of the heart. Finally, add the decorative border and droplet.

COLOUR PALETTE

PAISLEY PATTERNS

The classic Paisley design is a droplet-shaped leaf-type motif that originates in the Indian sub-continent, but takes its name from the Scottish town whose weavers adapted the design in the nineteenth century. The design is built up with concentric shapes, working from the inside outwards. The simple example on this page lends itself to a repeat pattern, like the fabrics created by the Scottish weavers. The second example on the facing page is more detailed, with a fringe of outer droplets.

scale drawing

This version of the paisley motif is ideal for use as a repeat design. Flip over the drawing to make a mirror image of the shape, then play around with fitting and intertwining the shapes in the traditional paisley manner.

COLOUR PALETTE

scale drawing

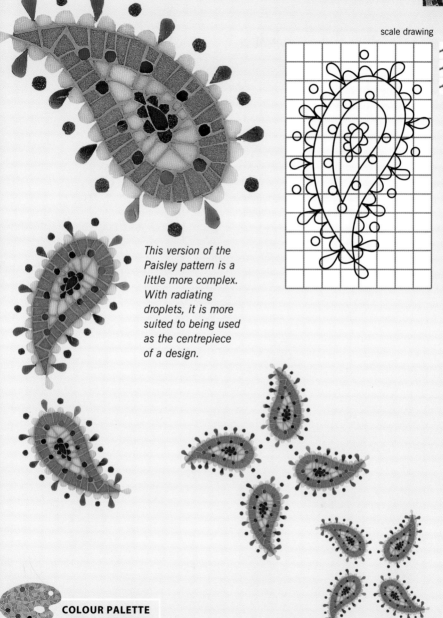

This version of the Paisley pattern is a little more complex. With radiating droplets, it is more suited to being used as the centrepiece of a design.

COLOUR PALETTE

BORDER PATTERNS

The borders featured here and on the following pages come from traditional Celtic, Roman and Moorish sources. Although centuries old, they can still be reinterpreted in new and interesting ways through imaginative use of colour. The borders can be used on their own to create a frame for a picture or mirror, but also look beautiful when used as an insert in a ceramic-tiled wall or work surface.

DIAMOND TESSELLATION

This diamond tessellation is simple to do as it mainly uses uncut tiles. You can radically alter the effect of this design by making the colours of the background closer to that of the foreground diamonds, by reversing the pattern (making the diamonds a light colour on a dark background), or by alternating the colour of every other diamond.

The slanted effect of this design works well either running across a background or surrounding a picture in which the tiles are laid in a vertical grid.

COLOUR PALETTE

Here a grout has been used in a shade between that of the design and the background. Colouring the grout to a tone closer to the background will add a different emphasis and make the design busier.

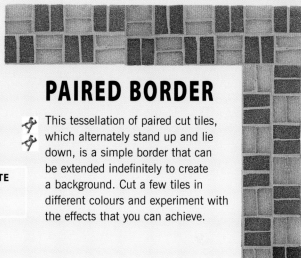

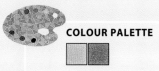

COLOUR PALETTE

PAIRED BORDER

This tessellation of paired cut tiles, which alternately stand up and lie down, is a simple border that can be extended indefinitely to create a background. Cut a few tiles in different colours and experiment with the effects that you can achieve.

SIMPLE ZIGZAG

A simple zigzag which, like the diamond tessellation, uses mainly uncut tiles. Experiment with drop shadow effects (see page 132) by using a slightly darker tone of the background tile immediately below the zigzag.

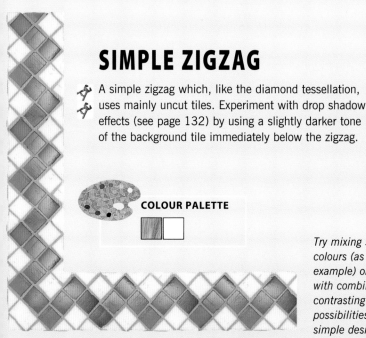

COLOUR PALETTE

Try mixing similar colours (as in this example) or experiment with combinations of contrasting colours. The possibilities of such a simple design are endless.

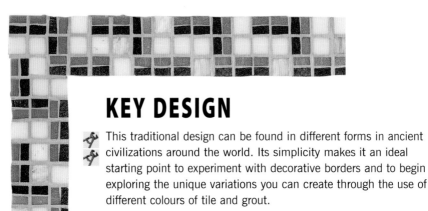

KEY DESIGN

 This traditional design can be found in different forms in ancient civilizations around the world. Its simplicity makes it an ideal starting point to experiment with decorative borders and to begin exploring the unique variations you can create through the use of different colours of tile and grout.

In this example, half tiles have been used to fill each block of the basic key design, allowing greater richness in the design. But as with the Zigzag below, the design can be rendered more quickly in whole tiles – a useful shortcut if covering larger areas.

 **COLOUR PALETTE**

ZIGZAG

Celtic motifs also include rectolinear designs like this one, and are often seen as borders in ancient manuscripts. They are certainly easier to attempt in mosaic, and can be varied by adapting the basic square grid through using halved tiles in a contrasting arrangement.

The simplicity of the zigzag pattern makes it ideal for creating long borders to add interest to tiled areas in the kitchen or bathroom.

COLOUR PALETTE

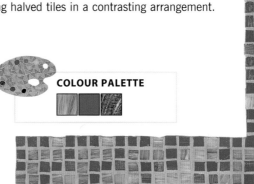

PYRAMID BORDER

At first glance, this design for a pyramid border seems to be one the simplest mosaics to achieve as every tile used is a square. However, to create this fine effect, each tile is a quarter of a whole tile – that's a lot of cutting, and probably a lot of spoilt tiles along the way, so you'll need a degree of patience.

Try complementary colour combinations (e.g. red/green or blue/orange) of similar tones to give a really vibrant effect to this border.

Before starting a decorating project, make sure that you have a sufficient quantity of tiles in the correct colours to fill the required area. It is surprising how many tiles even a short border can use.

COLOUR PALETTE

CELTIC SPIRAL

The spiral is a traditional Celtic motif which is interpreted here quite loosely with a predominantly monochrome palette, enriched with a few bronzed and golden tiles. For this motif to work, even when done in this way, it is important to scale the drawing and follow it quite carefully so that the overall effect is balanced.

scale drawing

When working on a circular design such as this, constantly rotate the baseboard or work around it from different sides of a small table so that you keep the tiling balanced and even.

COLOUR PALETTE

LARGE CELTIC KNOT

An ancient motif, often seen in jewellery and other decorative crafts. The symmetry of the piece makes it ideal for inclusion in a mosaic tabletop.

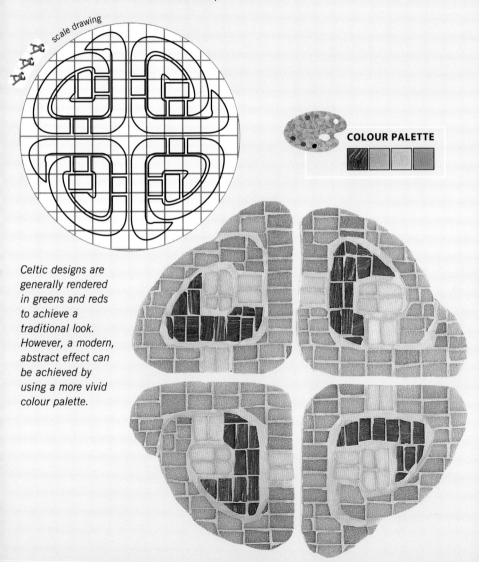

scale drawing

COLOUR PALETTE

Celtic designs are generally rendered in greens and reds to achieve a traditional look. However, a modern, abstract effect can be achieved by using a more vivid colour palette.

scale drawing

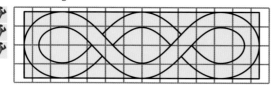

CELTIC ROPE

This traditional Celtic rope pattern is deceptively difficult to cut. The smaller the size of your mosaic, the more difficult you will find it to create a curve.

COLOUR PALETTE

In this version the design is made even more complex as each loop of the rope has an inner band of colour.

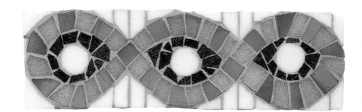

SMALL CELTIC KNOT

This motif, the 'triquetra', is the most basic Celtic knot design that can be seen in jewellery and ancient manuscripts, such as the *Book of Kells*. It is a motif that is pleasing when rendered simply and on a small scale, or developed more intricately as a larger piece.

scale drawing

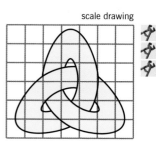

The knot is also ideal for use in repeated groups, in the manner of the heart designs on pages 80–81.

COLOUR PALETTE

CELTIC BOW

This is another quite complicated Celtic design – any motif that features lots of curves and swirls is a challenge to the mosaicist, requiring careful cutting, and probably resulting in quite a few rejects.

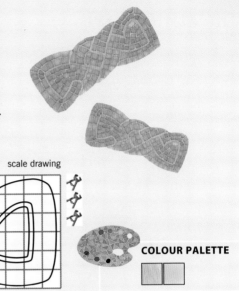

scale drawing

COLOUR PALETTE

Here the bow is a self-contained piece, but it can be repeated as a border by using fewer and simpler tile cuts.

Try alternating the colours of individual bows in a border, using two or even three different colour palettes.

ROMAN KNOT

This motif is taken from a Roman mosaic floor with clear Celtic influences. Here the design has been given a strong outline with more subtle, graded tones on the inside.

scale drawing

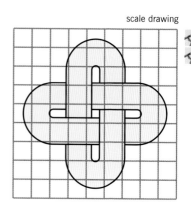

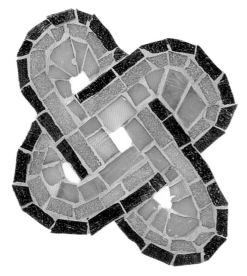

Follow the drawing carefully, particularly when trying to achieve the overlap effect of the knot, by using the outline only on parts of the design.

COLOUR PALETTE

ROPE DESIGN

Another rope design that you could find in Celtic art or nineteenth-century Art Nouveau. To create the tight curves you have to work on each and every tile and cut them accurately – if you leave uneven gaps and hope the grout will do the work for you, you will end up with a fragmented and unsatisfactory result.

scale drawing

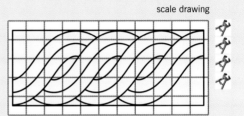

Every tile in this design has to be cut along each edge to ensure that the shape of the rope design flows successfully.

COLOUR PALETTE

DOTTY FLOWERS

scale drawing

The designs on these two pages are based on circles. They are hard work to cut, but the end results are effective and provide a different and flexible way to fill areas of your design in a fluid way.

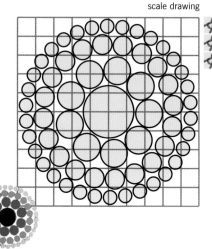

You may wish to work with ceramic tiles as these are easier to nibble and cut to circular shapes. You can also create the larger central circles in the design from a single piece.

COLOUR PALETTE

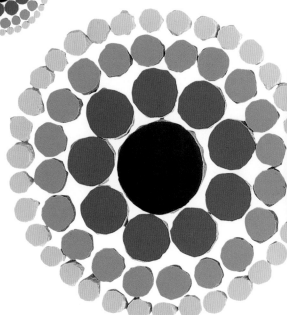

DOTTY STAR

This design has a strong focal quality, immediately drawing the eye to the centre. It is ideal for creating a busy background to a piece when repeated. Try the design in lighter colours against a dark background, perhaps darkening the tone slightly at the centre to emphasize the starburst quality.

This design is quicker to execute in ceramic tiles as they are easier to work to circular shapes and allow a greater range of sizes for each individual piece.

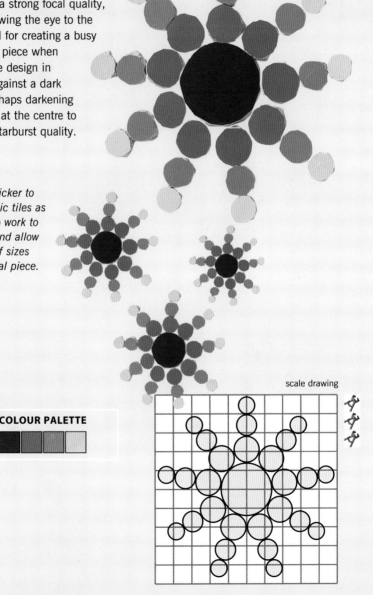

COLOUR PALETTE

scale drawing

SPRIGS

These sprigs provide a simple, relaxed motif
ideal for bordering an area of mosaic,
or to extend and repeat for a
background within a larger
mosaic design.

scale drawing

*Vary the design by
adding the leaves
in clusters or by
alternating the
numbers and
colours of the
berries.*

*The easy way to draw curves is
to use a large bowl or plate of
the correct size and trace round
part of its rim.*

COLOUR PALETTE

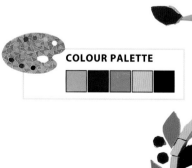

KNITTING

This piece is dedicated to my mother who was passionate about knitting. It is a motif which can be based on almost any pattern and design, and into which you could work in words and messages. It is also a decorative piece that could be done directly on to the lid of a sewing box or used as the surface of a work table.

Start by doing the knitting needles first, taking particular care to create the yarn loops around the needles. You can adapt almost any of the border designs in this chapter to make up the knitted garment itself.

scale drawing

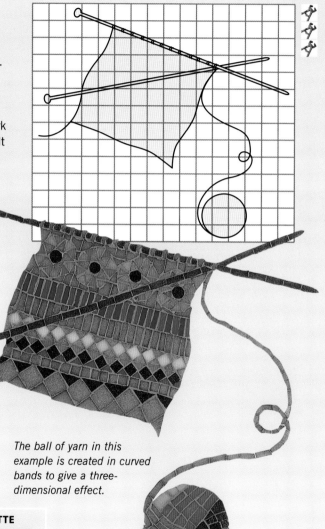

The ball of yarn in this example is created in curved bands to give a three-dimensional effect.

COLOUR PALETTE

CURVY PATTERNS

This pattern works well as a simple border or frieze, while the pattern on the facing page is more pictorial. Embellish as much as you like with leaves, flowers and organic shapes to complement the curves.

scale drawing

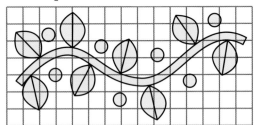

COLOUR PALETTE

You do not have to join each repeat in an identical way each time, particularly if you want a more natural effect.

To repeat the pattern for a continuous border, experiment with overlapping the stem of the design, so that each repeat flows smoothly from the adjoining one.

scale drawing

COLOUR PALETTE

The disjointed nature of this border design means that you can create a more varied effect, repeating the individual elements in different ways, or varying the spacing to produce a more fragmented, less rigid design.

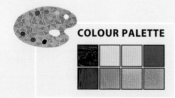

SYMBOLS

The sun and moon and the signs of the zodiac are potent symbols that are visually interpreted in contrasting ways in different cultures. They can also form the basis from which to develop very personalized pieces that combine an individual's star sign with an interpretation specific to their character and likes and dislikes. You can vary your interpretation of the designs in this chapter to match your own ideas about each sign and symbol and, if producing a piece for a friend or relation, add in colours and details that reflect their character.

SLEEPING MOON

This friendly moon – ideal for a child's nursery – is intended to have a soothing, luminous quality and can also be used as a companion piece to the smiling sun on page 102.

scale drawing

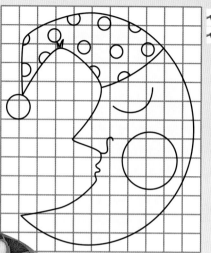

Start with the detail of the eye and the polka dots of the night cap, then work on the circular cheek. Finally, fill in the rest of the face If you wish, surround the face with a fine outline of small, darker tile pieces.

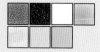

COLOUR PALETTE

SMILING SUN

This is a benignly smiling sun, with an Indian or Eastern feel. The shape of the bindhi on the forehead is echoed in the rays that surround the face. The cryptic expression recalls those seen in old Indian prints and wall paintings, whilst the shapes around the perimeter recall the roofs of temples and the palaces of the Raj.

scale drawing

This is a piece that has many possibilities for decorating further with paste jewels and sequins (see page 35).

MIX & MATCH

Partner this sun with the sleeping moon on page 101.

COLOUR PALETTE

ZODIAC WHEEL

This piece combines all the signs of the zodiac, which are shown in detail on the following pages. Use a pair of compasses to draw the circle, or draw around suitable plates and bowls to create the different circular bands of the design. Use a protractor to position the twelve long arms of the sun (the centres of which should be 30° apart from each other).

scale drawing

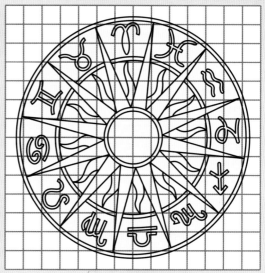

COLOUR PALETTE

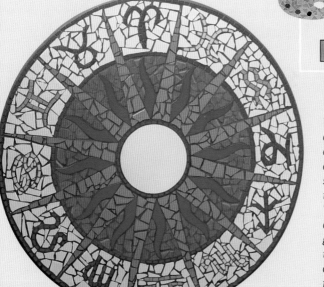

The intense red tiles combined with the crackled surround to each symbol give a sense of parched heat to this finished piece. The darkness and colour of the grout is a good choice, bringing together the flames of the sun, but further fragmenting the background.

SIGNS OF THE ZODIAC

The twelve signs of the zodiac can be interpreted in many ways. Here the character itself is drawn in solid, ink-black tiles to give a constant calligraphic effect. However, the backgrounds of each sign are given an interpretation of the month or the sign itself.

VIRGO

For the sign of Virgo, the background colours used here reflect the subtle shades of the grape harvest.

scale drawing

COLOUR PALETTE

Along with Taurus and Capricorn, Virgo is an earth sign so you could use colours from this palette for a very different look.

LEO

Leo is a fire sign – as are Sagittarius and Aries – so the use of such hot colours works well.

COLOUR PALETTE

Carefully follow the way individual tiles are cut to create the curves of this design. Try to avoid creating large gaps that will require heavy applications of grout, which would break up the flow of this glyph.

scale drawing

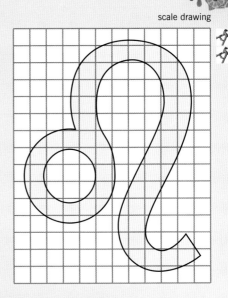

SCORPIO

As a water sign, an alternative for Scorpio would be to experiment with a blue colour palette. The shape of the motif, with its scorpion-like tail, also makes a more pictorial interpretation possible.

scale drawing

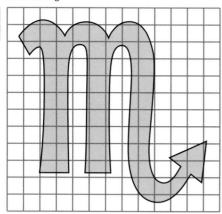

COLOUR PALETTE

Try to achieve the variation in thickness of the three strong verticals – they are slightly thinner in the middle and wider at the top and bottom.

SAGITTARIUS

The symbol for Sagittarius – representing a bow and arrow – plus the fact that this is a fire sign, could provide a very different interpretation in hot, violent colours.

The main shaft of the glyph needs to be as straight as possible. Tile this part of the design first, then add the arrowhead and stubs representing the bow afterwards.

scale drawing

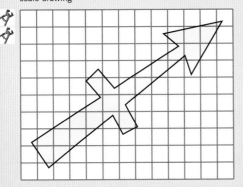

COLOUR PALETTE

LIBRA

Libra, the only inanimate sign of the zodiac, is rendered within its own stone arch. This is a very solid and balanced symbol, emphasized here by the curved tiling of the background that smoothly follows and encases the design.

scale drawing

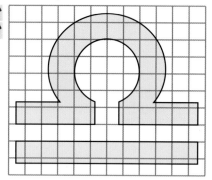

COLOUR PALETTE

As well as representing the scales or an 'equals' sign, the symbol for Libra is also said to depict the setting sun. You could experiment with a radiating background of orange fill to the centre of the motif to create a sunset effect.

CAPRICORN

Capricorn sits frozen, surrounded by the jagged icicles of mid-winter. This is perhaps the most intricate of the zodiac signs, and is said to represent the horns and tail of the goat.

scale drawing

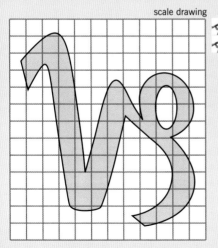

In this piece, a fragmented background has been used around the motif, suggesting cracked ice.

COLOUR PALETTE

AQUARIUS

Aquarius – a water sign – is rendered here in blue. The motif for Aquarius is also sometimes drawn as two curved zigzags for a more watery effect.

scale drawing

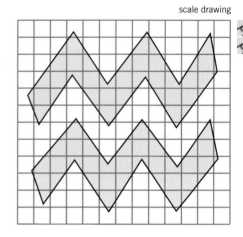

COLOUR PALETTE

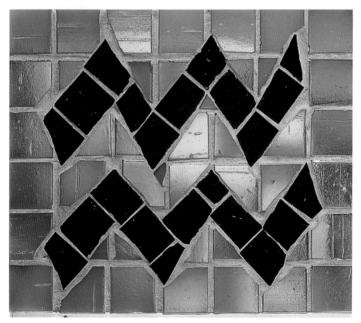

A uniform background of square tiles emphasizes the zigzags of this symbol.

TAURUS

The zodiac symbol for Taurus quite simply represents the head and horns of the bull. This Taurus sits on a field of blood-red tiles. The horns could be extended and weighted to give a more pictorial representation of the bull's head, even suggesting the bull's eyes by picking out tiles below the horns in a lighter tone.

scale drawing

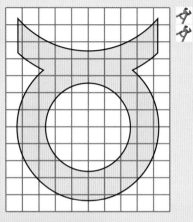

Great care has been taken to retain a strong symmetry when cutting the tiles for the symbol.

COLOUR PALETTE

PISCES

For Pisces, the background is sea green and reminiscent of fish scales. The symbol for Pisces represents two fish swimming in opposite directions, representing what is often regarded as an indecisiveness in Pisceans. It is important to achieve perfect balance in the shape and weight of the two vertical curved shapes.

scale drawing

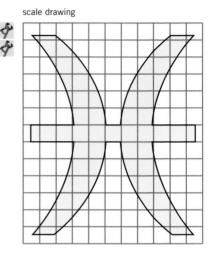

COLOUR PALETTE

This symbol could also be rendered in a more naturalistic way by adapting and mirroring the design of the angel fish on pages 166–167.

GEMINI

The symbol of two lines joined together represents the sign of the twins. Here the background has been made up of tiles split into opposing pairs, alluding to the fact that the relationship of the twins is not always harmonious.

scale drawing

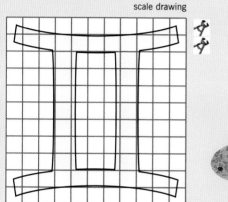

COLOUR PALETTE

Concentrate on creating both vertical and horizontal symmetry when you draw out the design for Gemini.

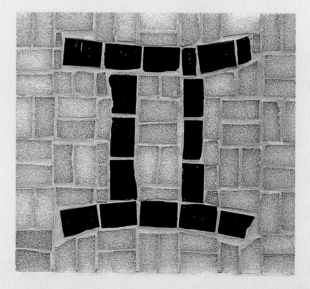

ARIES

Aries, the ram, is another sign represented with a very pictorial symbol of the horns of the animal. As with the other Zodiac symbols, it is important to establish the symmetry and balance of the sign when drawing the piece.

scale drawing

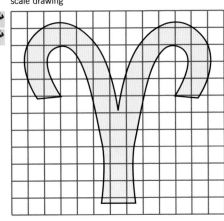

COLOUR PALETTE

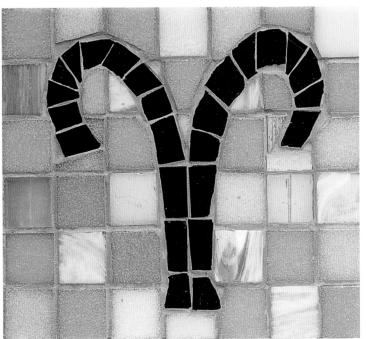

Here colours have been chosen to give the effect of a soft, woolly background, but a more combative feel could be given to this fire sign to suggest a character that greets the world head-on.

CANCER

In the Northern hemisphere Cancer, the crab, is the sign that coincides with the height of summer, hence the warm yellow background shown here. A water sign, it is also associated with nurturing and strength.

scale drawing

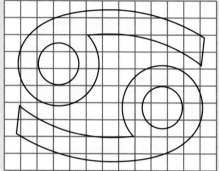

You need only draw up one of the claws of the symbol, transfer it, then rotate your drawing to repeat the shape for the second claw.

COLOUR PALETTE

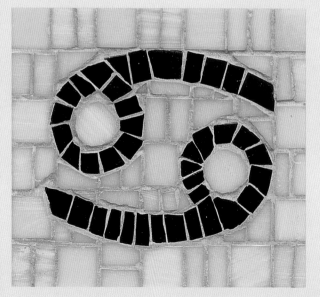

Here the symbol has been created with bright summer colours, but a watery palette would be equally appropriate.

LETTERS

Mosaic is a wonderful medium to produce unique signs and nameplates – for a room, a house or a business. Letters can be beautiful shapes in their own right and the variety of typefaces to use as inspiration is endless.

If you have a computer and printer, enlarge letters in a word processing program to the required size. For really big letters, enlarge each letter to the size of a sheet of paper. Your program may only show the letter size up to 72 points – about 2.5cm (1 inch) high. To make the letters bigger, type in a letter size of, say, 500 points. You can also format the font, turning it into an outline – this is easier to trace or cut round and reduces the amount of ink the printer uses.

The typeface used here was chosen for its bulk and solidity, making it ideal for mosaic tiling. Finer, more delicate typefaces can be used but require a lot more patience to interpret in mosaic.

This alphabet shows the different ways you can fill the letter outline. You can follow the letter closely, cutting each tile to hug the curves of the outline, such as in letter C. Alternatively, lay the tiles in a grid, cutting them at the edge to create the shape so the letter looks like a mask cut from a flat background, as in letter B. This method is ideal for pieces such as shop signs where ease of readability is desirable. Or simply treat the letter as an arbitrary shape to be filled with pattern and colour, as in letter J.

The colour palette selected also alters the final effect. Using colours that are similar in tone enhances readability, as in letter G, while clashing colours may increase decorative impact at the expense of readability, as in letter A.

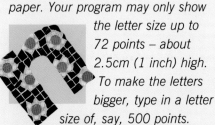

scale drawing

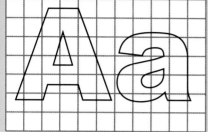

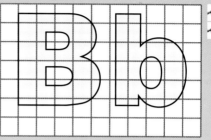

COLOUR PALETTE

COLOUR PALETTE

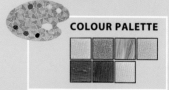

COLOUR PALETTE

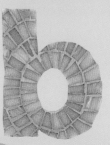

COLOUR PALETTE

scale drawing

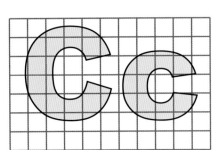

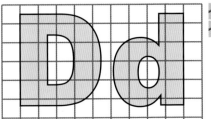

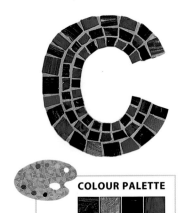

COLOUR PALETTE

COLOUR PALETTE

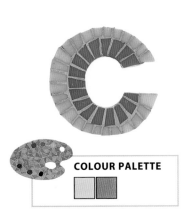

COLOUR PALETTE

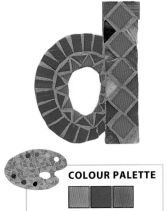

COLOUR PALETTE

scale drawing

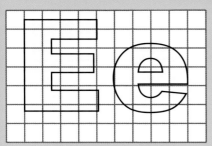
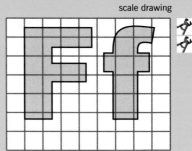

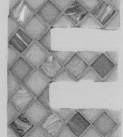

COLOUR PALETTE

COLOUR PALETTE

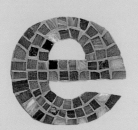

COLOUR PALETTE

COLOUR PALETTE

scale drawing

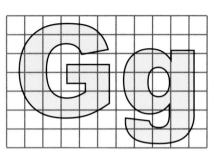 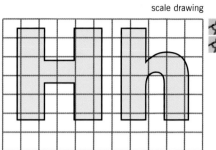

COLOUR PALETTE

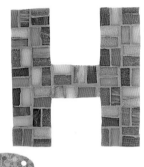

COLOUR PALETTE

COLOUR PALETTE

COLOUR PALETTE

scale drawing

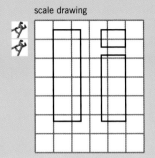

scale drawing

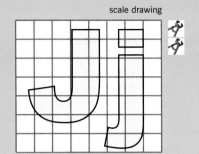

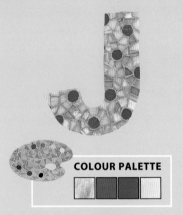

COLOUR PALETTE

COLOUR PALETTE

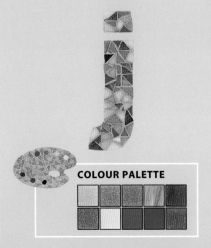

COLOUR PALETTE

COLOUR PALETTE

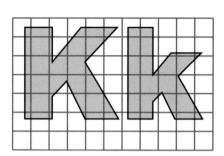

scale drawing

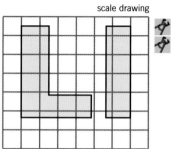

COLOUR PALETTE

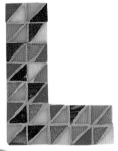

COLOUR PALETTE

COLOUR PALETTE

COLOUR PALETTE

scale drawing

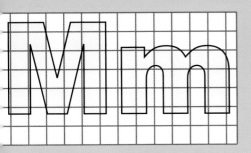

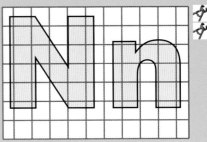

COLOUR PALETTE

COLOUR PALETTE

COLOUR PALETTE

COLOUR PALETTE

scale drawing

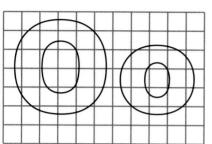

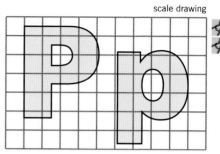

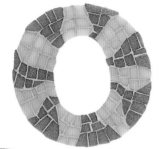

COLOUR PALETTE

COLOUR PALETTE

COLOUR PALETTE

COLOUR PALETTE

scale drawing

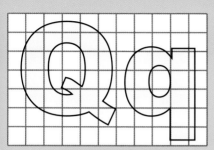

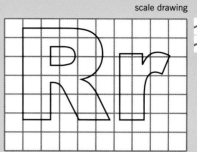

COLOUR PALETTE

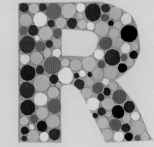

COLOUR PALETTE

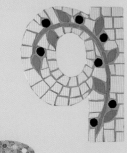

COLOUR PALETTE

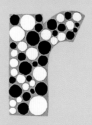

COLOUR PALETTE

scale drawing

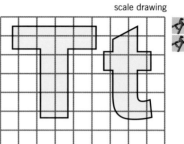

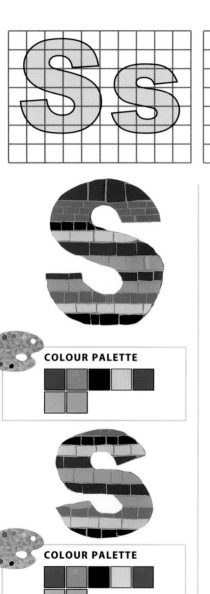

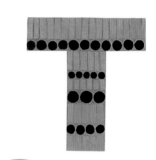

COLOUR PALETTE

COLOUR PALETTE

COLOUR PALETTE

COLOUR PALETTE

scale drawing

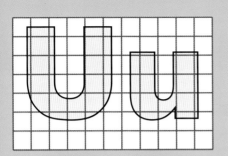

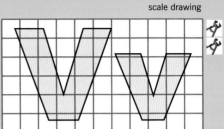

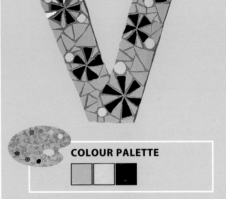

COLOUR PALETTE

COLOUR PALETTE

COLOUR PALETTE

COLOUR PALETTE

scale drawing

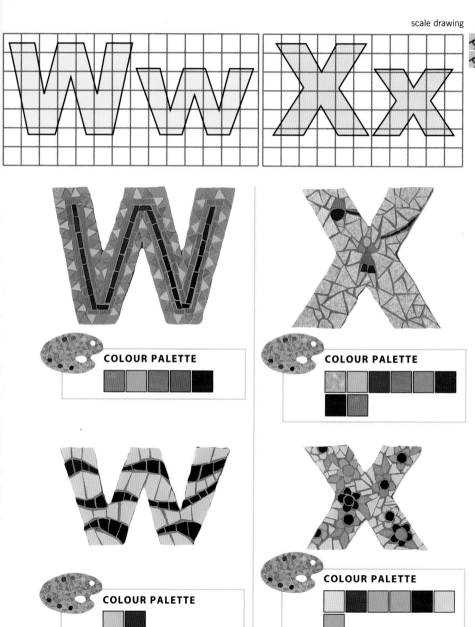

COLOUR PALETTE

COLOUR PALETTE

COLOUR PALETTE

COLOUR PALETTE

scale drawing

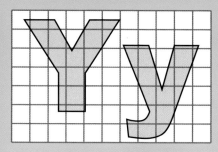

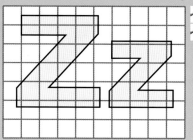

COLOUR PALETTE

broken tiles

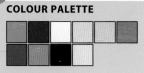

COLOUR PALETTE

COLOUR PALETTE

COLOUR PALETTE

COLOUR PALETTE

LETTERS WITH SERIFS

Serif letters are enhanced with decorative curls at the end of the main strokes and have an elegant, classic appearance. The alphabet illustrated here is an almost direct descendant from the lettering that inscribes ancient Roman monuments from the first century A.D. Here understated colours and simple building brick patterns have been used to retain the letters' classic beauty.

There is no point attempting these letters on a small scale – the proportions of the different strokes need to be rendered accurately and the curves of the serifs are almost impossible to cut if the letter is less than 10cm (4 inches) in height. Copy the letters carefully and fill their shape as neatly as possible. In these examples, household ceramic tiles have been used as they are easier to shape with the nibbling techniques described on page 54.

scale drawing

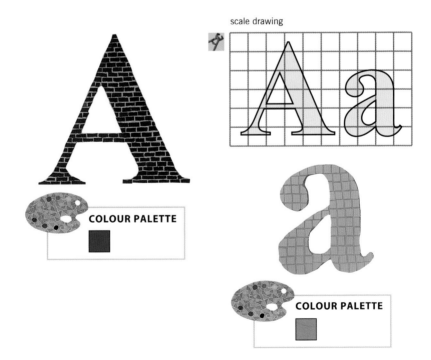

COLOUR PALETTE

COLOUR PALETTE

scale drawing

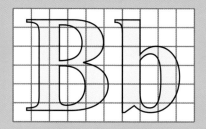

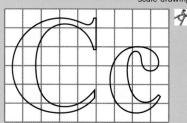

COLOUR PALETTE

COLOUR PALETTE

COLOUR PALETTE

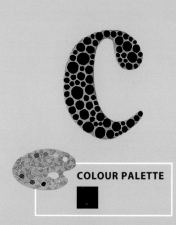

COLOUR PALETTE

NUMBERS

The numbers in these examples have all been made using only black, white and grey tiles. The end results show the variety of effects you can achieve just by varying the pattern of the tiles before you even introduce colour into a design.

As with the letters on pages 117–129, the tiles can follow the flow of the individual characters (as with the number 8), or be a flat design from which the number appears to be cut (as with the number 1), or just laid in apparently chaotic way (as with the number 5).

A simple yet very effective technique used here is the creation of a drop shadow around the numbers, giving a three-dimensional appearance, as if they are floating above the background. This is an easy effect to achieve, which you can use with many other designs.

Drop shadow

When you have transferred your design to the mosaic board, move the drawing a small distance (perhaps 1–2cm/^{1}/$_2$–1 inch) both down and to the side of where you have transferred the design to and retrace just the outline of the design a second time. Shade in the area between the original outline and this second outline, but only where this area is outside of the original outline. This is the area to be filled with the drop shadow tiles.

Use black or grey tiles for a graphic effect, but for a more realistic effect, the shadow should be a dark tone of any background colour surrounding the design (for example, if you have a red background, use very dark scarlet or even brown tiles for the drop shadow).

COLOUR PALETTE

scale drawing

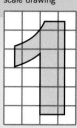

All the numbers in this section could be combined into a frieze for display in a child's nursery.

This outline effect is particularly useful in aiding readability when using the designs to create house numbers.

When using dots in a design, always start with the dot first and then fill round them, rather than leave gaps that will be difficult to fill accurately at the end.

scale drawing

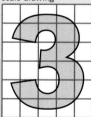

scale drawing

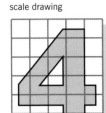

scale drawing

If using a stripe fill, draw these after you have transferred the outline to the baseboard, trying to balance the positioning of the stripes within the shape.

Crackle fills are an ideal way to use up tile fragments, but it can be time-consuming to find pieces that fit together without leaving too large a space for the grout.

scale drawing

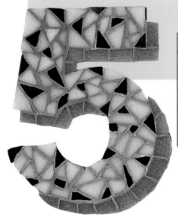

scale drawing

This type of fill works well if you use different shades of the same colour to hold the shape of the complete number together.

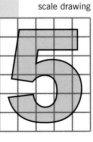

scale drawing

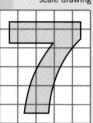

Begin tiling this fill by placing the semi-circular cut tiles on the inside of the figure first.

scale drawing

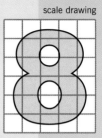

With this strong horizontal stripe pattern, start with the longest stripe running across the top of the number. Spacing stripes with a gap that is slightly wider than a tile (or half a tile) makes cutting and filling the design much easier.

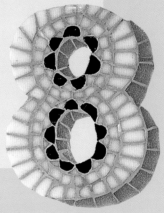

scale drawing

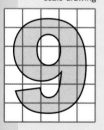

This design is a reversal of the design of the number 6 on the opposite page, but also consider using closer tones of the same colour.

scale drawing

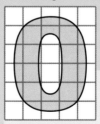

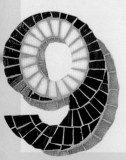

Complete each flower shape first, then fill the spaces in between.

SPECIAL CHARACTERS

Symbols and special characters can be treated in exactly the same way as letters and numbers. Opposite, the dollar symbol has been given a stars and stripes treatment – you might think of other illustrative fills for particular words and phrases when creating signs for homes or businesses.

scale drawing

This hash symbol works well if you cut tiles with a diagonal slant to match the slope of the symbol.

COLOUR PALETTE

scale drawing

COLOUR PALETTE

The ampersand is not only a convenient device to reduce numbers of letters required in a sign, but it is also a pleasing shape in its own right. You can extend the shape to entwine other elements in your design, for example, the initials of a couple or a group of children.

scale drawing

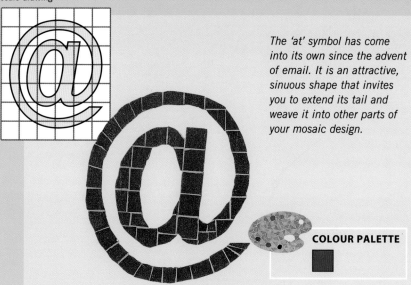

The 'at' symbol has come into its own since the advent of email. It is an attractive, sinuous shape that invites you to extend its tail and weave it into other parts of your mosaic design.

COLOUR PALETTE

scale drawing

Experiment with different humorous fills for the dollar symbol, for example, try cutting ellipses from metallicized tiles to create a pile of coins.

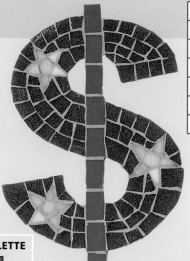

COLOUR PALETTE

ANIMALS AND BIRDS

Animals and birds are always such popular motifs with almost universal appeal. On the following pages you will see a range of treatments ranging from the naturalistic, where tiles and colours have been chosen to give a life-like effect, through to highly stylized designs where an animal is used almost as a caricature of its shape or size.

FOX

This mosaic captures the alert nature of the fox, combining dark and light tones. It's a chunky mosaic that doesn't take long to create, but is very effective.

scale drawing

To create the impression of fur, cut the tiles into small, ragged, oblong shapes. Mix tiles in several shades of brown, rust, and terra-cotta to add texture to the fur.

COLOUR PALETTE

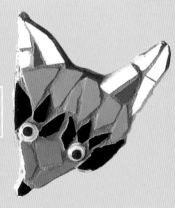

MIX & MATCH

Use this design with the fox cub on page 157, to create a woodland scene.

scale drawing

INDIAN ELEPHANT

Despite its simplicity, this is a popular motif – the animal has a solidity and beauty with a twinkle in its eye. If you wish, add to the design by sticking jewels or sequins to the elephant's harness (see page 35).

The elephant's blanket is the starting point for this piece. Other motifs from this book would work just as well in this part of the design.

COLOUR PALETTE

After completing the blanket, proceed with the face, tusks and the details of the feet, before filling the remaining bulk of the elephant's body.

SPOTTY ELEPHANT

This is a cartoon interpretation of the animal's shape to give a charming effect with coloured polka dots.

scale drawing

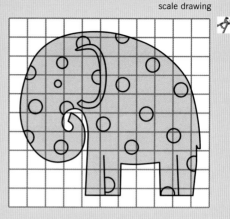

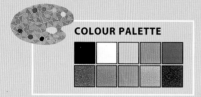

COLOUR PALETTE

Start with the polka dots, the eye, and the outline of the ear, before filling the remainder of the design.

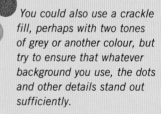

You could also use a crackle fill, perhaps with two tones of grey or another colour, but try to ensure that whatever background you use, the dots and other details stand out sufficiently.

VERY EASY CAT

Just 14 tiles, simple cuts, gives you . . . one cat. Job done!

scale drawing

Using glass mosaic tiles inevitably means that the end result is a very small version of this motif, although one that can be repeated and mirrored to give a pleasing border design.

COLOUR PALETTE

This piece can also be created using larger household tiles, and given a jazzy effect by including patterned tiles or selecting a clashing range of plain tiles.

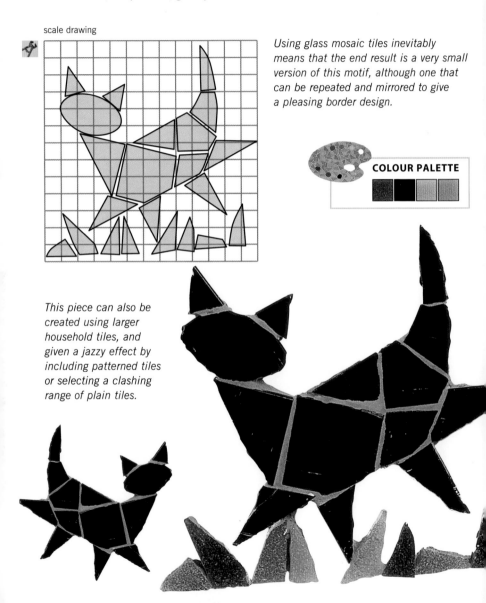

DEER

This design of a deer retains a strong, naturalistic quality, whilst being heavily stylized. The elongated legs give a powerful sense of the speed and also the delicacy of the galloping deer.

The tiles follow the natural coloration of the deer quite closely, but the colour palette used is much richer and deeper.

Take particular care when tiling the legs of the animal to retain the delicate quality of the design.

scale drawing

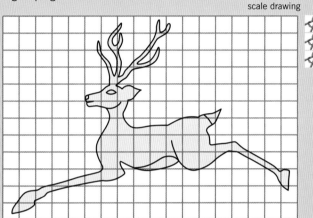

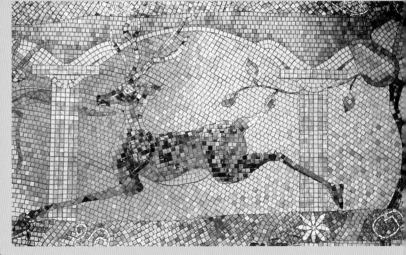

COLOUR PALETTE

SCOTTY DOG

A cute motif of a popular dog that is almost a silhouette, apart from the colours of the body warmer, which has been given a tartan pattern. Using long, thin tiles gives the sense of the shagginess of the fur.

scale drawing

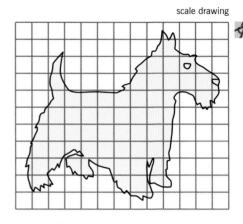

You could work a set of initials into the Scotty dog's body warmer (see pages 117–129), or use any one of the motifs from the Patterns and Borders section on pages 76–99.

COLOUR PALETTE

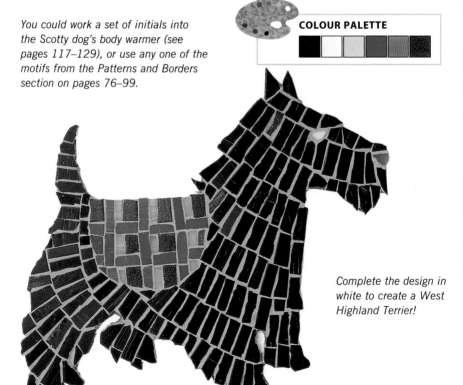

Complete the design in white to create a West Highland Terrier!

PINK POODLE

The poodle was a popular design motif in the 1950s, which gives this mosaic a kitsch, retro feel. Exaggerate this by using the most vivid pinks you can find, and cutting the tiles in circles to give a bubble effect.

COLOUR PALETTE

scale drawing

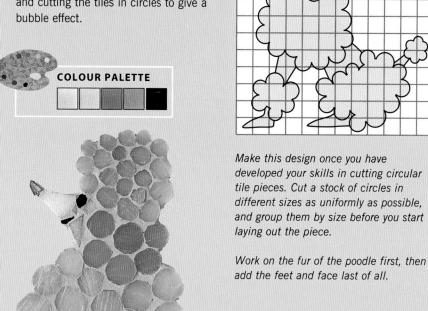

Make this design once you have developed your skills in cutting circular tile pieces. Cut a stock of circles in different sizes as uniformly as possible, and group them by size before you start laying out the piece.

Work on the fur of the poodle first, then add the feet and face last of all.

For a really kitsch effect, add decorative bows to the tail or head, or make the piece in shades of blue.

TOUCAN

The toucan's stark plumage and powerful, colourful beak make it instantly recognizable. This 'over the shoulder' pose makes for a denser design. Work outwards from the eye and the beak first – positioning the smaller pieces of mosaic required for these details is easier on an empty surface, rather than trying to fit them in later. In this example the plumage has been realized using contrasting black and white tiles with a few mid tones. You could experiment with blues and bottle greens.

scale drawing

Create a background of crackle-patterned green tiles or realistic leaves and branches around the bird.

Glue on a 'googly eye' (see page 35) to give the bird an even more exaggerated beady-eyed look.

MIX & MATCH
You could lengthen the toucan's perch to create a tableau including the Macaw on page 148.

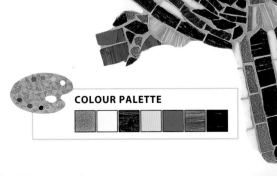

COLOUR PALETTE

EAGLE OWL

This piece uses a similar palette of tiles to the Native American figure (see page 219) and has the same feeling of a design created in wood or bone. Start from the shoulders of the bird and work down each feather, cutting the neighbouring tiles to roughly the same shape and size and from similar tiles. Position the eyes and ears carefully to achieve a symmetrical effect, otherwise you may end up with an unintentionally comic face.

scale drawing

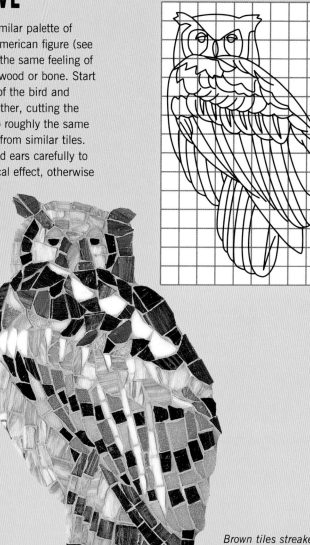

Tile each feather vertically, but take care not to align the different colours and tones horizontally or the shagginess of the plumage will be replaced by harsh, unrealistic stripes.

COLOUR PALETTE

Brown tiles streaked with gold or copper colours give the feathers a rich and realistic texture.

MACAW

Although the softness of feathers is the very opposite of the hard-edged feel of ceramic tiles, mosaic actually works very well in rendering the sense of a bird, like this Scarlet Macaw. Use the brightest tiles to give the vibrant sense of the bird's plumage – you can follow a naturalistic design, or, if you prefer, take liberties and experiment with more raucous colour combinations. Pay most attention to the face of the bird where the tiles give a sense of the mechanical strength of the beak.

scale drawing

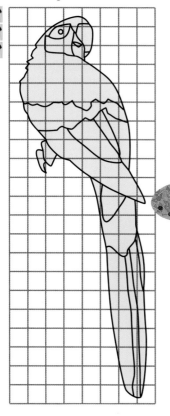

This macaw does not necessarily need a background as it has a compact shape which is relatively easy to cut out with a jigsaw. Always cut your baseboard to the shape of the outline before you commence tiling.

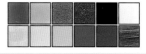

COLOUR PALETTE

Tile each feather vertically, trying to follow the width fairly smoothly.

This piece would look good displayed in a conservatory or hung behind a suitable grouping of indoor plants.

COCKEREL

This stylized, non-naturalistic cockerel draws its inspiration from Russian folk art. In this example, different areas of the plumage are filled, almost arbitrarily, with flower and leaf motifs. Almost any pattern from a folk art tradition could be used – hearts, other animals or even human figures.

scale drawing

Start with the detail pieces, such as the flowers, circles and leaf motifs.

Use a thick baseboard, cut to the outline shape, to create a trivet or hot plate stand for use in the kitchen.

Note the banding of the tiles around the middle of the body, giving the bird shape and form.

COLOUR PALETTE

SNAIL

First draw the outline and then the
contours that give the shape of the
snail's shell. Try to follow the drawing
carefully when placing the tiles.

scale drawing

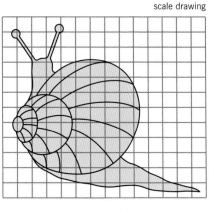

*Follow the drawing
carefully to create bands
within each section of
the shell.*

*Tile each section of the
shell in the bands to
create the roundness
of the shell.*

*Pearlescent tiles are best
for giving a naturalistic
appearance.*

COLOUR PALETTE

BUTTERFLY

The shape of the butterfly can be used and interpreted in so many ways. Here circular patterns have been used, working outwards from the centre and gradually filling the outline.

   If you want a more naturalistic butterfly, visit a library and look at books about these wonderful creatures to get more inspiration from nature's colour and variety.

In this example ceramic tiles have been used to give larger pieces and finer control of the shapes.

scale drawing

Whatever design you use, the important thing is to retain the symmetry of the butterfly's wings. The trick is to draw the design for one wing, then flip the drawing over, and use a light-box (or hold the drawing to a window) to trace it in reverse to give the design for the opposite wing.

MIX & MATCH

This design would make a nice jungle companion piece to the Toucan or Macaw on pages 146 and 148.

COLOUR PALETTE

TWO LOVE BIRDS

A pretty decorative motif that you can adapt through extending or varying the patterns below the birds and by adding decorative materials, such as sequins or diamanté, as in this example. This is an ideal piece to make a plaque to commemorate a wedding or engagement, perhaps working in a date or adding the couple's names into the design.

scale drawing

To ensure symmetry, scale up just one bird and half of the heart, transfer this to the baseboard, then turn the tracing over and use it to create the facing side of the design.

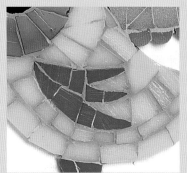

Start by tiling the fine detail of the design – the eyes, wings and centre of the heart.

The diamanté beads are applied with a strong glue, but do not use these if the piece is to be used for a functional purpose, such as a table top, which will subject the decoration to wear and require washing.

COLOUR PALETTE

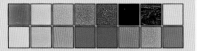

MIX & MATCH

Use this motif with a background or border incorporating the spirals on pages 78–79.

SITTING CAT

Cats are always a popular motif, and this simple design can be rendered in a stylized or naturalistic way using different colour palettes The spiral of the tail, cutting across the banded stripes of the cat's body, is a feature which you can develop using contrasting colours and grouts.

scale drawing

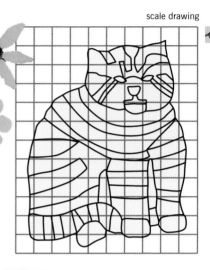

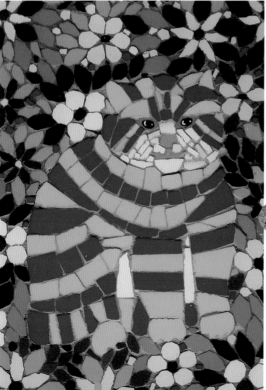

Here a dark grout is used which gives the reds and oranges an added lustre and picks out the tiles without fragmenting the design.

COLOUR PALETTE

AZTEC LIZARD

The distinctive zigzag lines and diamond patterns on the lizard's back give this mosaic a South American flavour. This is a striking design that would work very well on a patio table.

scale drawing

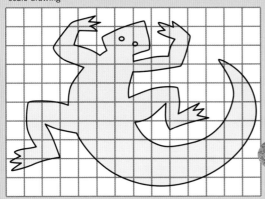

The strong outlines and the bright colours dispersed evenly throughout the lizard emphasize the flatness of the design.

COLOUR PALETTE

Tile the outline first and then draw a strong central spine from which to work the fill around, to ensure the finished piece is well balanced.

An alternative colourway would be to use more earthy tones – browns, ochres and reds – perhaps almost submerging the design into a similarly coloured background created with a crackled, random fill.

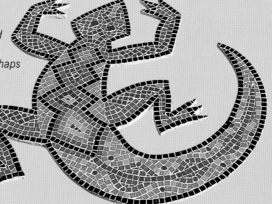

BEE

The bee is a simply
rendered motif that
can be used at a
small scale to add
a highlight to a flower
picture or larger motif.

*Simplify the design even
further, cutting each
element of the bee's body as a
single tile or china fragment, and
discarding the legs and antennae
altogether. Glue the tiny bees to
a terracotta flower pot to create
your own 'honey pot' in
which to plant bright
summer flowers.*

scale drawing

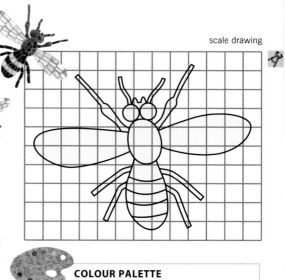

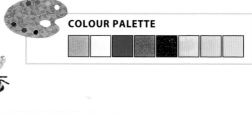

COLOUR PALETTE

FOX CUB

This relatively simple design uses large pieces of tile fragments to create a light, almost wind-blown feel. The subtle gradation of the tiles chosen adds to the rich naturalness of the picture, even though the different elements are treated almost abstractly. On this occasion, a plain white grout is a sensible choice to complete the piece.

scale drawing

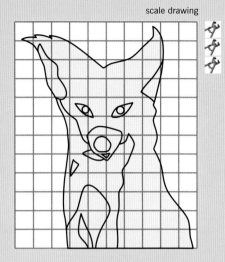

As with any animal motif, the positioning of key features, such as the eyes and nose, is crucial if the end result is to be effective.

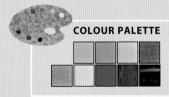

COLOUR PALETTE

STAG

Caught in mid-leap, this stag has the air of a mythological beast – strong, even slightly malevolent. Only a few almost monochrome colours are used to enhance this effect.

scale drawing

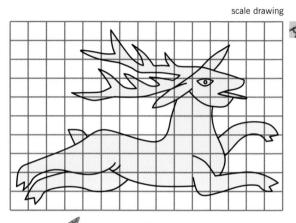

The cuts of the tiles are straightforward but give a flowing, powerful and very pleasing finished design.

COLOUR PALETTE

PENGUINS

These loveable birds are suited to mosaic
with their stark, contrasting, almost abstract
plumage which works well against a strong
background of almost any colour.

*ile the birds
irst, working
ut from the
ye, then work
he background
round and
etween them.*

scale drawing

COLOUR PALETTE

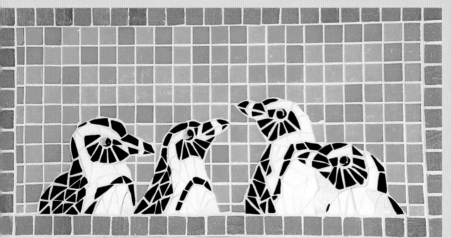

*A naturalistic background of cool ultramarines makes
the design ideal for use in a watery environment,
such as a shower room or swimming pool.*

BULL

Similar in style to the stag on page 158, this bull is more a minotaur than a barnyard beast. Appearing solid and fierce due to the strong, dark outlines, this piece is simple to cut and you will have little difficulty achieving this splendid end result.

scale drawing

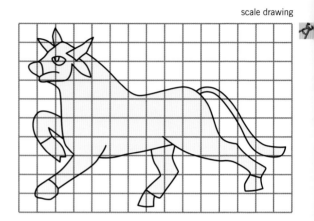

COLOUR PALETTE

GOOSE

This is a simple but strong design that would work well for a trivet, or repeated in a frieze above a kitchen worktop with other farmyard creatures. The design has been enhanced with a small butterfly 'gem', attached to the background with a small dab of glue.

scale drawing

COLOUR PALETTE

Begin the mosaic by working the eye and the wing, then fill in the other details.

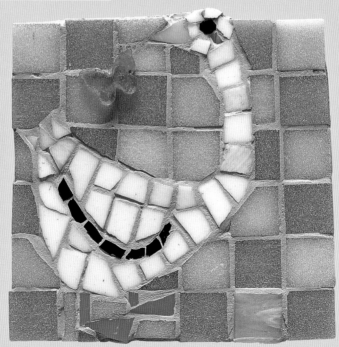

MIX & MATCH
Combine this design with the colourful cockerel on page 149.

DUCKS

This is a mosaic reworking of the traditional flying ducks that adorned living room walls in the 1950s. You could easily make a series of different-sized ducks. The duck seen below uses a naturalistic palette, while the examples on the facing page show how you can let your imagination run wild.

scale drawing

Make a rough tonal sketch before you cut the tiles, so you can plan the relevant colours for different areas.

COLOUR PALETTE

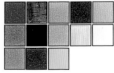

COLOUR PALETTE

Use large ceramic kitchen or bathroom tiles to achieve large, flat areas of colour.

This flower-power interpretation is a more psychedelic working of the same design, featuring a central flower.

COLOUR PALETTE

MARINE LIFE

Sea-life has provided inspiration for mosaic designs dating back to ancient Roman times, no doubt due to the use of mosaics in buildings such as bath houses and laundries which have an obvious association with water. Many of the designs in this chapter lend themselves to similar use, perhaps as a decorative splash-back in a bathroom or kitchen, or to provide a decorative feature in a swimming area. However, do remember that if the finished piece needs to be waterproof, it is vital to use the correct grouts and, most importantly, if the piece is to be displayed in an outside area, the materials must be able to withstand the extremes of weather, particularly frost.

DOLPHINS

This pair of playful dolphins, mirrored around Neptune's trident, reminds you instantly of the mosaics found in the bath houses of ancient Rome.

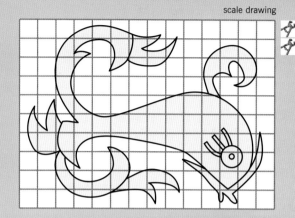

scale drawing

Use a single drawing and turn it over to provide the tracing for each dolphin.

The background fill around the dolphins rigidly follows their outline and adds to the visual completeness of the piece.

COLOUR PALETTE

ANGEL FISH

These mosaics use the same colours for each of the three fish, becoming paler in tone as they decrease in size. This is an easy piece to attempt with lots of possibilities for different use of colours and patterns. The shape is easy to draw and fill, and the results are effective with either a basic, bright set of colours or a deeper and more complex palette. The angel fish work well as a small decorative piece, or use as a large wall-sized mural in a bathroom.

If you want the finished piece to be cut to the outline of the fish, trace the drawing to a suitable baseboard and then cut using a jigsaw. Make a number of cuts from the edge to cut away the waste between the fins and tail – don't try to follow the outline in a single cut, or the saw will jam on the corners of the design.

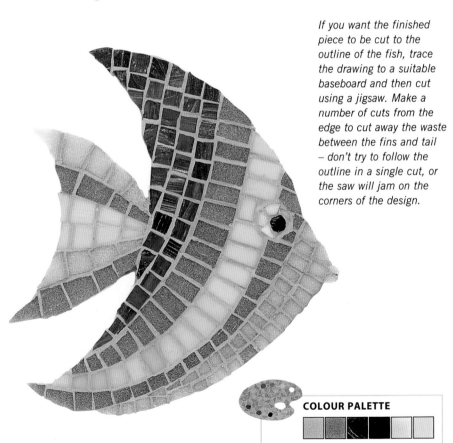

COLOUR PALETTE

The exotic, almost electric colours of tropical fish give you plenty of scope to experiment with different colours and any number of the metallized or pearlescent tile finishes that are now widely available.

scale drawing

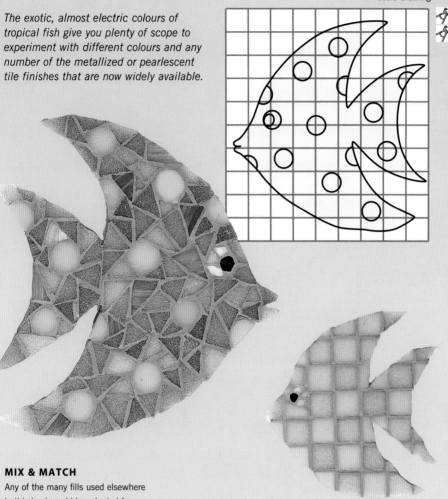

MIX & MATCH

Any of the many fills used elsewhere in this book could be adapted for use with this piece. Have a look at the alphabet section on pages 116–131 for alternative ideas for fills, or you could adapt the drop shadow technique used in the numbers section on page 132 to raise the fish above a background.

GOLDFISH

In shape and proportion this design is quite realistic. However, the use of a bright colour scheme enhances the geometric quality of the fish. Using glassy or pearlescent tiles, in this example on the face, gives a translucency to the finished piece.

scale drawing

When preparing the drawing, you might want to divide the body of the fish into bands to lay the rows of scales between to give a three-dimensional effect to the fish.

COLOUR PALETTE

The eye is always a crucial, focal detail for a piece like this, so be prepared to take several attempts to cut the central circle and surrounding tiles exactly right.

Pre-cut the shapes of the scales and the triangular tiles that separate them in batches so that you can play with different combinations to get the best fit .

SEAHORSE

Mosaic tiles are an ideal medium for communicating the faceted brittleness of the seahorse. Note how the pieces along the backbone have been notched to increase the scaly effect.

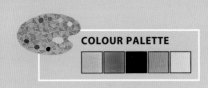

COLOUR PALETTE

A brown colour palette could be used to give the seahorse a more naturalistic feel.

scale drawing

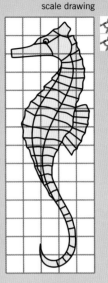

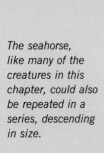

Start with the backbone of the seahorse and be sure to give the tail a generous curve.

The seahorse, like many of the creatures in this chapter, could also be repeated in a series, descending in size.

CONCH SHELL

This motif follows the colours and patterns typically found on shells collected from the beach. The tiles have been cut very carefully to give an organic, flowing effect.

scale drawing

You could create your own design from shells collected from the beach.

COLOUR PALETTE

Pearlescent tiles add a richness and realism to this design.

Start with the darker areas, nibbling the tiles with tiles nippers to get softer, curved edges. Then fill the areas in between with fragments for lighter tiles.

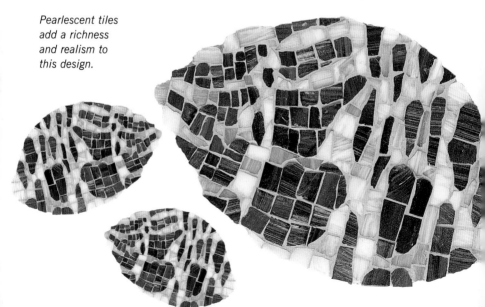

SEASHELL

Exaggerated pink hues and pearlescent tiles have been used to create this shell. You could experiment with other shapes and use shells found on the beach for inspiration.

scale drawing

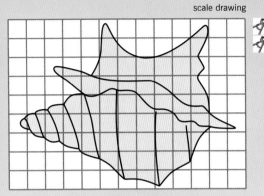

COLOUR PALETTE

Softer, lighter colours are used for the inside of the shell.

MIX & MATCH

You could use the shell as a seat for the mermaid on page 220.

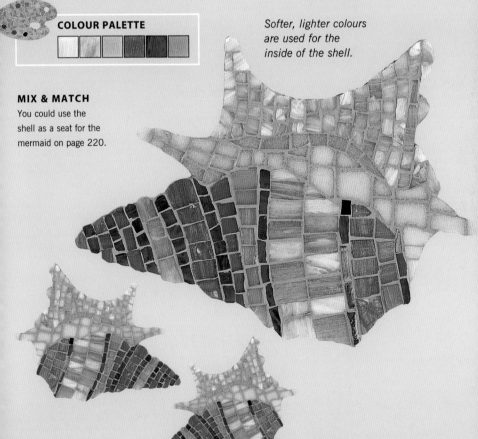

STARFISH

Very much a beginner's piece, this stylized starfish is a great starting point on your mosaic journey. The colours used here suggest the sea: natural greens, blues and yellows. To add more details, cut the tiles into smaller fragments and continue the dots of colour into each of the arms of the starfish.

scale drawing

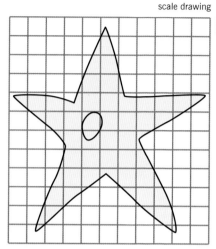

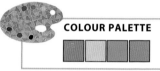

COLOUR PALETTE

Mosaic the star design first, starting with the central dot, then continue with the simple square-cut tiles for the frame. Finally, fill in the background area.

WINKLE SHELL

The seashore offers up endless examples of nature's beauty. Any shells can be used as inspiration: exaggerate their strong shapes and their variations in colour and pattern.

scale drawing

COLOUR PALETTE

The natural, gentle shades of this mosaic are rendered by the deep red touches.

When working on designs with a strong organic feel, draw curved lines as guides which you can follow to keep the flow of the tiles to suggest the curves and shape of the object.

The background of this mosaic is interesting as it outlines the shape of the shell but also has a watery feel.

DOLPHIN CIRCLE

The acrobatic dolphin leaping from the waves or carrying a human on its back is an image passed down from ancient times. This design is ideal for a frieze or a tabletop.

scale drawing

COLOUR PALETTE

Use a long ruler and a protractor on your baseboard to draw out spokes on which to lay each dolphin. You could place between four and eight dolphins depending on how large you want them to be, but if you want to alternate the two different designs then you must use an even number.

The circle of whole tiles around the outside of the design provides an attractive and neat finish and prevents sharp, cut edges facing outwards if the piece is to be used as a tabletop.

SEAGULL

The source for this design was an illustration in an old book. Whilst the interpretation may not be strictly accurate to an ornithologist, the fullness of the wings and care with which the feathers have been cut and placed to flow in line give the bird a realistic feel.

scale drawing

Pearlescent tiles and a rich, though subtle, variation in the colours of the plumage help prevent the design from becoming flat or dull.

As with most bird designs, preserving the delicacy of the legs is vital to achieve a good finished result.

Start with the head, then lay the tiles in the direction away from the head to give the feathers a backward sweep.

Try to emulate the shadowing on the underside of the bird.

COLOUR PALETTE

NURSERY

Mosaic lends itself so well to the nursery because its bold colours and shiny texture make it attractive and eye-catching for children. The mosaicist can really let their imagination run riot to produce cute or fantastic objects without being restrained by adult ideas of decorative taste.

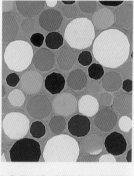

scale drawing

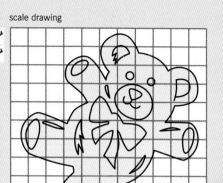

TEDDY BEAR

A children's favourite, this motif makes a lovely picture for a nursery. You can elaborate and personalize the bow and the facial expression. In this example, 'googly eyes' of the type found on novelty toys and cards have been added. It makes an ideal companion piece to the rag doll on page 184.

The teddy's eyes are stuck on using strong craft glue.

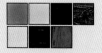

COLOUR PALETTE

You could personalize the bear by replacing the bow with a child's initial (see pages 117–129).

scale drawing

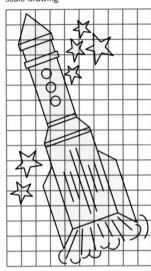

ROCKET

This space rocket is a shape and colour extravaganza which owes more to psychedelia than NASA. However the work involved is perhaps deceptive, particularly if you follow the bubble-powered design of the main stage of the rocket.

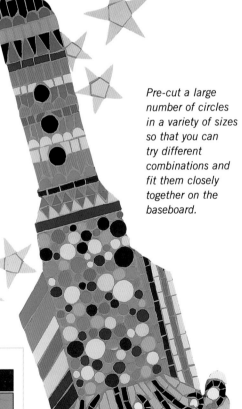

Pre-cut a large number of circles in a variety of sizes so that you can try different combinations and fit them closely together on the baseboard.

MIX & MATCH
You could use the spirals on pages 78–79 to create a background of swirling fireworks.

COLOUR PALETTE

STEAM ENGINE

Very much a beginner's piece, this train is simple to draw and the design will not suffer if you are not completely accurate with the positioning of the tiles. If you can make all the wheels sit on a pencil line, the effect will be more grounded. Treat it as a fun piece to play with colours and develop your tile-cutting skills.

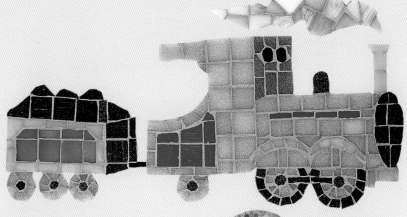

Personalize the piece with an initial or name running along the side of the engine and its tender, adding extra carriages if need be. Alternatively, add some of the other motifs from this section, such as the teddy or rag doll on pages 177 and 184, as passengers.

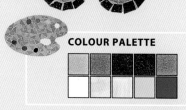

COLOUR PALETTE

scale drawing

Use spirals, stars, or other motifs if you want to create an unusual steam cloud from the funnel.

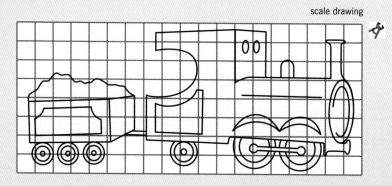

FLOWER FAIRY

A pretty piece that works well on a small scale. Use the hair and the flower as a mask to avoid the difficulty of trying to create facial details. The pearlized tiles give a transluscent feel to the figure. Try creating a frieze of different fairies combining the colours of different flowers with the shades of the skirt.

Mosaic the flower in the fairy's hair first, then fill in the rest of her hair.

scale drawing

You could also create this piece using larger ceramic tiles, cutting the petals of her dress as single pieces of tile.

COLOUR PALETTE

IMP

A companion piece to the flower fairy on the facing page, although this character has the opposite nature and an air of mischief. The wings of the imp have been cut from mirror glass. Take care working with this material as it is liable to shatter and give sharp edges. You should wear gloves and safety glasses when cutting glass and also finish the edges by rubbing them with glass paper if they are going to be left exposed. 'Googly eyes' have been stuck to this imp, to add to his naughty appearance.

Start with the fine detail – the face and the dots of the toadstool – then fill in around them.

scale drawing

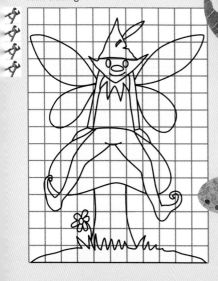

Graduate the colour on the toadstool's stalk to give a three-dimensional effect.

COLOUR PALETTE

MONOCHROME DINOSAUR

This dinosaur requires intricate cutting to achieve the detail and to communicate the three-dimensional form of the animal. Look carefully at how three different tones have been used to give highlights and shadows. By using a different colour palette of greens or olive tones – but still with three distinct tones – a more 'realistic' effect could be achieved.

scale drawing

COLOUR PALETTE

Try to keep the clean, sweeping curve of the neck, back and tail when you scale the drawing on to the baseboard.

RED DINOSAUR

This follows the same drawing as the dinosaur on the facing page, but is flipped in the opposite direction. This is a large piece suitable for the beginner as it uses a large number of uncut tiles. Note, however, the cutting of some critical tiles to achieve the sweeping shape of the tail.

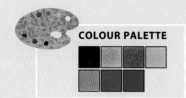

COLOUR PALETTE

This simpler version of the dinosaur has had a child's initial worked into it. Use any combination of the letter outlines and different fills from the alphabet section on pages 117–129.

You could add a background of trees, perhaps dwarfed by the dinosaur to emphasize its size.

scale drawing

RAG DOLL

This is a pictorial piece that stretches the strict definition of mosaics. Ceramic tiles have been used to allow the plain shape of the bodice to be created from a single piece. The head was cut as a simple oval, then the hair and features painted using oven-fired ceramic paints.

COLOUR PALETTE

In this example, real buttons have been glued to the bodice.

The fullness of the skirt is achieved by following a gentle curve along the bottom hem. The folds of the material have been suggested by splitting and slightly offsetting some of the flower motifs.

scale drawing

CLOWN

This piece draws from the make-up of Coco the Clown, with white surrounding the mouth and eyes, painted, hooped eyebrows, and, of course, the red nose (with a single piece of tile providing a highlight).

Take care cutting the tiles for the eyebrows to graduate their thickness.

Note the slight curvature to the 'crosses' of the eyes, and the graduation in the tones of the hat to give dimensionality.

COLOUR PALETTE

MIX & MATCH

You could add a colourful spotted bow tie, copied from the teddy bear on page 177.

SWINGING MOUSE

A fun piece for a nursery
wall and very simple to
tile. Add a child's initial
to the kite to personalize
it (see pages 117–129
for letters).

scale drawing

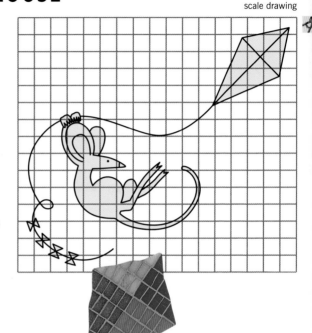

MIX & MATCH

Change the design on the kite
by using flower motifs from the
Borders and Patterns chapter on
pages 76–99.

*When working on
the string, keep
the tiles thin and
positioned in a
straight line.*

COLOUR PALETTE

BALLOON

This hot-air balloon works equally well as part of a landscape tableau or as a stand-alone piece.
The large area of the balloon offers countless possibilities to personalize and adapt the design.

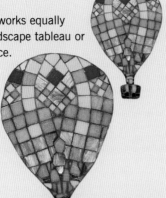

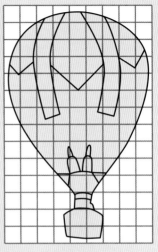

scale drawing

Add further guidelines to your drawing to help you create tapered bands of tiles and to ensure a symmetrical end result.

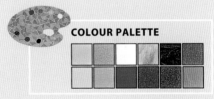

COLOUR PALETTE

The bright yellow bands give this balloon a really strong shape – look at how the tiles are carefully tapered and curved on the outside edges.

FOOTBALL

Football produces fanatical supporters, even at a young age. This piece allows you to create a strongly personalized gift for the young football fan. The circular shape also makes it ideal as a tabletop if scaled up sufficiently.

scale drawing

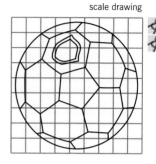

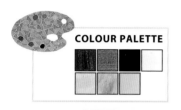

COLOUR PALETTE

In this version a club badge has been reproduced within the design. Alternatively you could create the ball in the team's colours if the badge is too intricate.

Take time to look at the way the pieces of the ball work, with a pentagon surrounded by a ring of hexagons.

Instead of plain white tiles, flat pieces of old crockery have been used to add interest. The dark grout is important in holding the finished design together and the grout lines between the main shapes of the ball have been left a little wider to emphasize their outline.

DANCING JESTERS

These figures have the acrobatic, almost elastic quality of circus characters or puppets. In your drawing, keep the disjointed feel to the limbs and a delicate, pointed feel to the legs.

scale drawing

The stripes on the leggings run vertically for one figure and horizontally for the other. You could also experiment with polka dot fills, reversed for each character.

COLOUR PALETTE

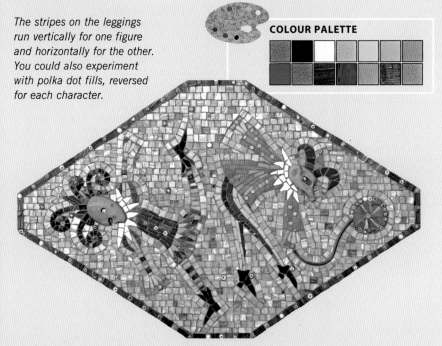

The background tiles follow the outline of the figures for a single tile depth, then change to a more even, flat fill to add interest to the piece.

FLOWERS AND LEAVES

In this chapter, flowers and leaves provide inspiration for a number of motifs that range from the simple, to the highly complex. Whether naturalistic or fantastic, these designs can convey a whole range of moods. With these motifs you are free to choose colours from anywhere in the spectrum, so the range of possibilities is endless.

SIMPLE FLOWER

This is probably the simplest of the flower motifs in this chapter, and is an ideal beginner's piece. If you cut out the baseboard to the outline before you begin, then the piece is very practical and can be used as a trivet in the kitchen or as a stand for a flower vase.

scale drawing

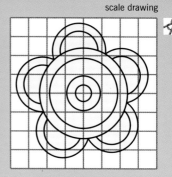

Draw the circles of the design with a pair of compasses or, alternatively, use upturned plates or bowls as templates.

Start tiling from the central dot, working your way outwards, completing each ring. Then do each petal before finishing the piece with the outline tiles.

Produce a series of flowers in different colours, and experiment with the colour of the grout. Try colouring grout so that it contrasts strongly with some areas of the design but is similar to other areas of tiles.

COLOUR PALETTE

DAISY

The basic drawing for this cheerful daisy is very simple and, as with all the flower designs, feel free to vary the size and shape. It is very easy to change the proportions of the flower without it looking wrong.

scale drawing

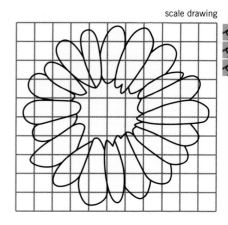

If you wish, you could make the daisy petals from one piece of tile, rather than several smaller fragments.

COLOUR PALETTE

Yellow grout used here gives a pollen-dusted appearance and unifies the petals with the yellow centre.

TROPICAL FLOWER

The shape of this flower gives
a languid effect, helped by the
way that single ceramic tiles have
been cut for each petal.

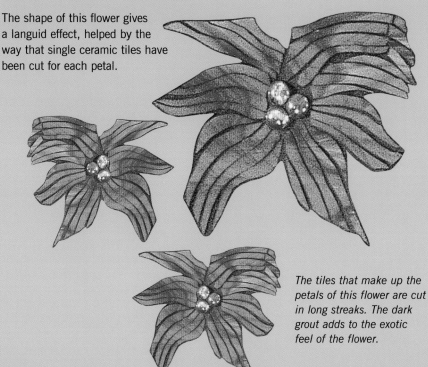

*The tiles that make up the
petals of this flower are cut
in long streaks. The dark
grout adds to the exotic
feel of the flower.*

scale drawing

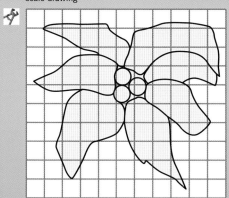

MIX & MATCH

This flower would work well with
the stylized flower featured on
page 197.

COLOUR PALETTE

CLIMBING FLOWER

This simple floral motif is embellished with curly fronds, which make it ideal to extend and entwine with other elements in your design, or to create a delicate and intricate repeat pattern.

scale drawing

Draw out the fronds and work out how to interconnect them with each other if you are doing a repeat design.

Tile the flower head first, then tile the fronds. Experiment with a range of tones for these.

COLOUR PALETTE

scale drawing

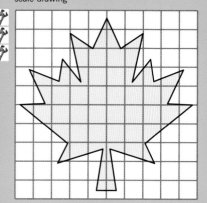

MAPLE LEAF

The maple leaf is a strong, recognizable shape that works equally well when given either a naturalistic or abstract treatment.

With all leaves, the symmetry of the shape is vital.

COLOUR PALETTE

Repeat the motif on a small scale to make an attractive border. You can also adapt the design to provide a background or frieze, overlaying the design in different sizes and positions in an arbitrary manner to create a carpet of leaves.

scale drawing

SUNFLOWERS

Sunflowers, with their densely packed, shaggy petals and seed-laden centres, are instantly recognizable. This motif works well on a large scale, matching the size of the real plant, perhaps as a wall mural or as a tall, thin panel.

Here a naturalistic palette has been followed, but with an impressionistic use of dabs of bright colour. Look at the many pictures of sunflowers painted by Vincent van Gogh for inspiration, to enhance and develop your own version of this motif.

COLOUR PALETTE

STYLIZED FLOWER

This design uses carefully cut individual petals to give an effect like a small fire with leaping flames.

The drop-shaped tile, in a deeper shade of purple, provides a central focus to the flower.

COLOUR PALETTE

scale drawing

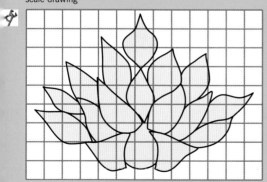

VASES OF FLOWERS

These vases of flower designs are different workings from the same master drawing. The top tip for all these flower pieces is to use a backing material – such as tile mesh or even paper – on which to create each individual flower on. Glue the pieces for each flower to its own separate piece of backing and allow to dry, then carefully cut away the excess backing from around the tiles. You can now move the individual flowers around on the baseboard and work out their exact position before gluing them down.

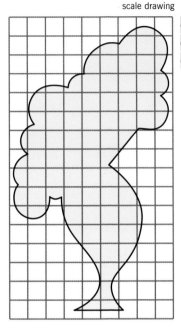

scale drawing

Use any of the individual flower motifs from this section to fill the vase, or combine a mixture of designs. Start by looking at the details on pages 204–205.

This is a bright and stylized interpretation; the vase is brimming over with exuberantly coloured flowers in concentric circles, vying for attention, almost like a firework display. The asymmetrical vase adds to the fun, informal feel.

COLOUR PALETTE

The same design has been given a more naturalistic treatment using sunflowers – an homage to Vincent van Gogh's obsessive paintings of the subject. The centre of each sunflower varies and is cut to different sizes – take a look at a flower book or seed catalogue to see the large number of different sunflower varieties available. The vase has been given a tonal gradation to provide depth and dimension.

This flower is an alternative form of the sunflowers on page 196.

COLOUR PALETTE

This third treatment has a retro feel that harks back to 1950s fabric and ceramic design. The rose is made up of the same sequence of shaped tiles laid in an interlocking group (see detail on page 205). This rose motif can be adapted as a repeat pattern to fill other objects or to create a lush background to another design.

These relatively simple cuts using deep-coloured tiles create the convincing impression of the head of a rose. A black and white stripe would be an alternative to the polka dots.

COLOUR PALETTE

ORNAMENTAL GRASSES

This is a pleasingly simple design in its basic form, here made slightly more challenging by cutting the pot as thin shards of graded tones of the same colour to give three-dimensional form.

The grasses or flowers are made up of thinly cut tiles, placed in lazy curves upward from the pot and adorned with a few circles and simple, abstracted flower heads to lend an airy, stylized feel to the design.

An alternative treatment for the vase would be to mosaic it in mirror tiles.

COLOUR PALETTE

GARDEN FLOWERS

Here is an alternative treatment to the ornamental grasses on the facing page, with louder, more stylized flowers and a warmer colour palette.

scale drawing

Play with the proportions of the vase at the drawing stage.

Tile all the flower heads first, then create each stalk.

Note the colour graduation in the vase to give a three-dimensional effect.

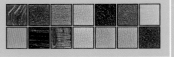

COLOUR PALETTE

CLOVER AND FERN

These simple organic shapes lend
themselves to being used as borders or as
a decoration to combine with other motifs.

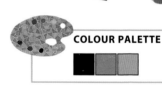

*The fern can be
given a lush, jungle
interpretation, making
it ideal to combine with
motifs such as the
Toucan or Macaw
on pages 146
and 148.*

*The clover
works well in circular
clusters. Add as many
leaves as you want or
keep to the traditional
four of the Irish
shamrock or lucky clover.*

COLOUR PALETTE

scale drawing

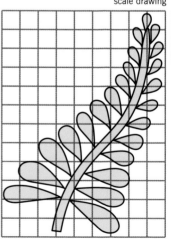

TULIP

This is a strongly stylized, almost geometric interpretation of the spring flower. Reverse and alternate the design to make a decorative border or background fill.

scale drawing

COLOUR PALETTE

As with all flower designs you can invent your own palette. Try frosty pinks or deep purples against sweeter, apple-green backgrounds.

FLOWER DETAILS

The simple motifs provide a reference
for you to adapt and use in other pieces
elsewhere in this book (such as the vase
designs on pages 198–199).

scale drawing

*Start by carefully cutting
a circular centre, then cut
a number of petal shapes.
Position these by eye to
get the result you want
before beginning to
glue any of the
tiles in place.*

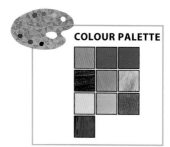

COLOUR PALETTE

scale drawing

COLOUR PALETTE

This is a close-up of the rose motif used in the flower vase at the bottom of page 199.

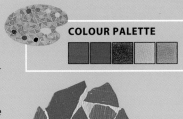

scale drawing

Cut and play with all the petals of each flower head before you start gluing the tiles. It is important not to be too rigid about following a drawing. Trust your own eyes to give you the best result.

COLOUR PALETTE

FOUR SEASONS

This idea of the seasons could be applied to other designs, for example a house or a landscape. Start by working on the shapes that are common to each design in the series, in this case the tree trunks. Try to cut and position them as accurately as possible so that they match in each frame of the sequence. Then fill in the elements that are different for each season – here the leaves, blossom and fruit.

You could use very different background colours for each season (rust colours for autumn, apple-green for spring, etc) or embellish each version of the image with figures or birds and animals.

This series has been cut from ordinary household tiles (see page 34). The advantage of using these tiles in this particular design is that elements like the tree trunks can be created from larger tile fragments. These tiles are also easier to shape, using nibbling techniques to get the common elements in each frame the same size and shape.

scale drawing

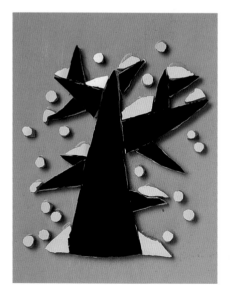

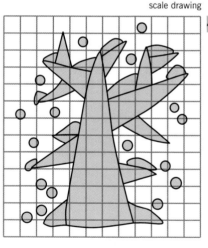

When cutting the snow shapes, try to soften and curve the edges as much as possible to give the effect of drifting snow.

COLOUR PALETTE

Cut the blossom circles as small as your skill and patience allow.

scale drawing

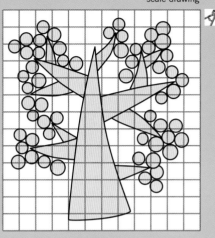

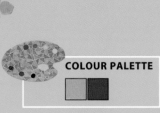

COLOUR PALETTE

A sprinkling of one of the flower motifs from page 204 could be added around the base of the tree.

scale drawing

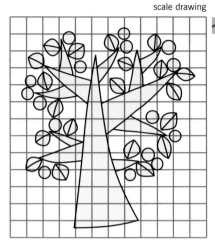

COLOUR PALETTE

For the summer tree, select colours for whichever fruit you want. You could even try cutting lemon shapes or clusters of tiny fragments to represent cherries.

A repeat pattern allows you to create a seasonal border or frieze. Alternatively, you could lengthen the sequence of steps to show the change during the seasons of the year.

scale drawing

COLOUR PALETTE

Cut lots of leaves in shades of rust, brown, and orange, then play with their position to create the effect of falling leaves. If you are really ambitious, you could try curving the shape of the main trunks to give the effect of strong winds bending the trees.

FIGURES

Representing human figures provides one of the biggest challenges to the mosaicist. The details of facial expression or the delicacy of hands and fingers are difficult to render in cut tiles. It is often the case of giving an impression of the human form – the overall shape and posture of the figure are what you need to convey – so concentrate on drawing the figure accurately and retaining the proportions.

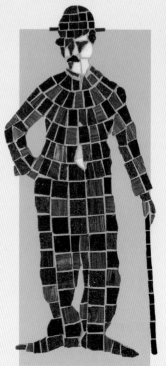

BALLERINA

This design depicts a classical ballerina posing on her points. For the design to work, take special care with your drawing to get the poise and balance of the figure. Use a ruler to draw the strong line of the standing leg and back, and the diagonal of the arms. Then fill out your drawing around this armature.

scale drawing

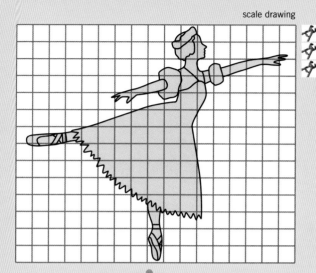

Start tiling the tutu from the top and work down to give a full, flowing effect. When cutting and laying the tiles, pay particular attention to the size and shape of the standing foot.

Delicate pinks and creams make an ideal palette, but you could experiment with stronger colours.

COLOUR PALETTE

ART NOUVEAU PORTRAIT

With her chignon and curls, this picture harks back to the style of the 1970s, which itself drew on the romanticism of turn-of-the-century Art Nouveau designs. The piece is an example of how mosaic is so suited to adapt a picture or illustration through the use of a patterned fill. Many of the motifs in this book could be developed in the same way, by taking a flat area of the design and filling it with a pattern of your choice.

Pay attention to your colour palette: in this example, although the colours are quite exotic, they have been selected to balance each other, and care has been taken to spread the colours and tones evenly over the patterned area.

It is worth cutting and laying all the tile pieces in the design, and experimenting with their position before you begin gluing them to the base. Note how the flat tiles of the face follow the contours of the jaw, neck and nose.

scale drawing

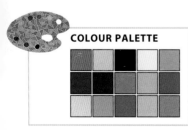

COLOUR PALETTE

JAZZ LADY

The inspiration for this piece came from a sheet music cover from the jazz era. The character is a 'Good Time Gal' who has seen better days. The heavy eyes and lashes, green eye-shadow and orange hair add to the garish feel of the motif.

This mosaic was created using ceramic tiles. A strong sweeping feel is achieved by using large pieces for the boa and other background elements.

The lips are cut from glass mosaic tiles to give a strong central point of focus to the face.

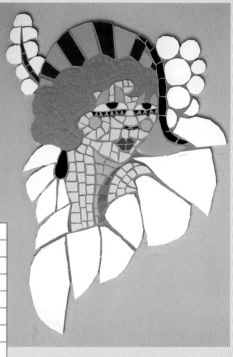

scale drawing

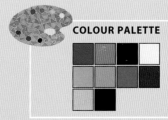

COLOUR PALETTE

AUDREY HEPBURN

Holly Golightly, immortalized by Audrey Hepburn, was the central character in the classic film, *Breakfast at Tiffany's*. Although this treatment of the portrait is monochrome, brown rather than black tones have been used to give the image warmth and depth. Pearlescent tiles have been used for the necklace, tiara and earrings.

scale drawing

Start with the eye, nose and mouth detail, then fill in the skin tones. Be prepared to make many attempts to cut some of the crucial detailed tiles, such as the highlights in the eyes, to get these exactly right.

This piece uses a technique of posterization, where an image is divided into a small number of basic tones (in this drawing, three) which are drawn out on the baseboard. Carefully select and sort your tiles into these three tonal groups before filling each area. You can vary the colours of the tile within each area, providing they are as close as possible in tone.

COLOUR PALETTE

JAPANESE LADY

The kimono is a Japanese design with a long and complex tradition. This interpretation is a simplified version that uses blocks of colours and stylized floral designs. The pose of the figure, taken from a seventeenth-century print, has an air of mystery, suggested by the pancake whiteness of the face and the slight turn of the head.

Care must be taken when grouting the pieces as the tiny eye and mouth detail can get lost.

scale drawing

MIX & MATCH
Use other designs from the flower motif section on pages 204–205 to decorate the kimono.

COLOUR PALETTE

CLASSIC PORTRAIT

The treatment of this face draws heavily on the techniques of classical Roman and Byzantine mosaic with its inclusion of strong outline elements dividing different areas of the face. A strongly stylized piece, it is nonetheless very expressive. Look at ancient mosaics in historical reference books for inspiration, and to study their use of colour.

scale drawing

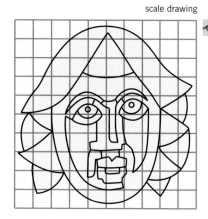

Work on the outline first using evenly sized pieces of tile, or even whole tesserae if you are producing this on a larger scale. Then fill in the areas in between the outlines, either with flat areas of tiles, or, as here, contouring the tiles around the outlines.

Use different colours of tiles for the hair, to create a feeling of movement and life.

COLOUR PALETTE

SCARECROW

The scarecrow is a familiar figure in the rural landscape worldwide, recorded by Shakespeare and immortalized in the film *The Wizard of Oz*. This scarecrow is a simple, thin, windblown figure. Vary the scarecrow's wardrobe and, if you like, place him in a landscape, surrounded by a flock of crows. The scarecrow would also provide a different basis for the Four Seasons designs on pages 206–209.

scale drawing

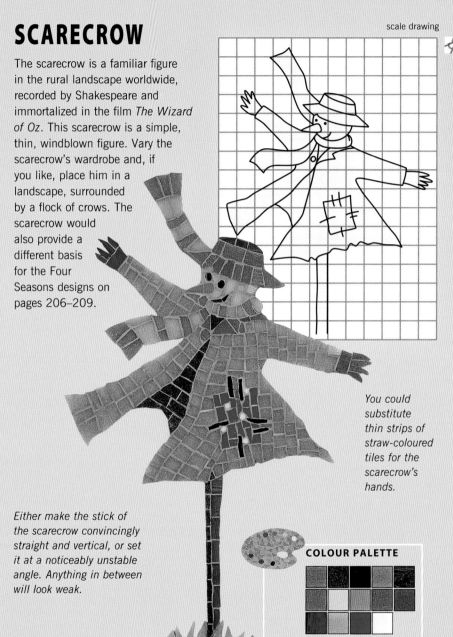

You could substitute thin strips of straw-coloured tiles for the scarecrow's hands.

Either make the stick of the scarecrow convincingly straight and vertical, or set it at a noticeably unstable angle. Anything in between will look weak.

COLOUR PALETTE

CHARLIE CHAPLIN

The outline of the silent movie star Charlie Chaplin is instantly recognizable. However, whilst this piece uses very dark tones, they are not all solid black, thus avoiding a flat, silhouette effect. The tiles of the body are cut in a patchwork, reinforcing the idea of the tramp. The tiles increase in size as you move down the figure to give a more comic, pear-shaped feeling to the figure as a whole.

scale drawing

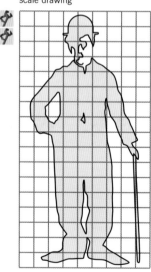

Take particular care in cutting and positioning the cane, as it is important in establishing the weight and balance of the piece.

COLOUR PALETTE

NATIVE AMERICAN

Rendered in profile, this portrait is almost a silhouette. Mixing dark brown tiles flecked with metallic gold and ivory coloured tiles gives the effect of marquetry. This effect could be heightened by cutting the tiles even smaller, and filling out the areas of the design in more rigid lines.

scale drawing

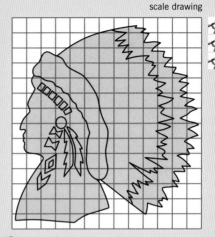

An alternative would be to use a strong Navajo palette of colours, such as blues and oranges, as a different decoration for the head-dress.

COLOUR PALETTE

MERMAID

This mermaid appears to be half-fish, half-seaweed. The tiles for the hair are cut in small oval shapes to give a sense of disarray, while the tiles for the tail are cut in the shape of fish scales, following the shape of the tail and tapered towards the end. The scales are graded tonally to give a sense of dimension. If you wish, you could position the mermaid on a rock, or use different effects to render an underwater background. You could also experiment with a non-naturalistic version, using a brighter colour palette.

scale drawing

Another alternative for the tail of the mermaid would be to tile this with fragments of mirror glass.

MIX & MATCH

Combine this motif with a choice of shells and fishes from the Marine Life chapter to make a decorative splash-back in a bathroom.

COLOUR PALETTE

FLAMENCO DANCER

scale drawing

This figure has the fiery colouring and haughty poise of the flamenco dancer. Like the ballerina on page 211, getting the posture and balance of the figure in your drawing is vital for the piece to work. You will see that the outline of the figure has an exaggerated curvaceousness. The arms have also been made slightly longer than real life to emphasize the dancer's pose, with a two-tone treatment to render the skin tones.

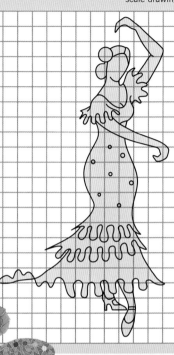

The rose in the dancer's hair is a miniature version of the examples on page 205. You could add more in a mixture of colours.

COLOUR PALETTE

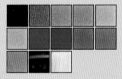

Position the polka dots on the dress first, then fill the material around them. Notice how the tiling of the skirt follows the contours of the hips to add to the curvaceousness of the dancer.

MARILYN MONROE

This is an advanced piece, requiring a degree of experience to render the face at this scale. From that point of view, the larger you make the piece, the better. Use different shades of white for the skirt – pearlescent tiles give a sense of the material's lightness and movement. An iconic piece for a movie buff, this mosaic works well when the whole piece is shaped to the outline of the figure, rather than as a rectangular picture.

scale drawing

Tile Marilyn's eyes, nose and mouth first, taking great care with the famous pout.

Choose the colour of the grout carefully so as not to lose any features in the finished piece.

COLOUR PALETTE

scale drawing

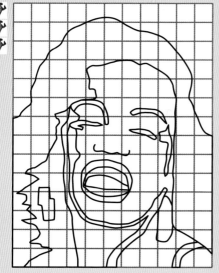

There are some faces that are so iconic they are recognizable even when described visually with just a few lines or shapes. Marilyn Monroe is one such face and, with some care, it is possible to portrait her in mosaic.

Play around with tile fragments until you find the exact colours for the skin tones. If you take particular care with the finer details – the eyes and mouth – then the other areas of the portrait will look after themselves and the end result will be breathtaking.

COLOUR PALETTE

Like the portrait of Audrey Hepburn on page 214, the drawing divides the main areas of the piece into simple areas which should be tiled in consistent tones.

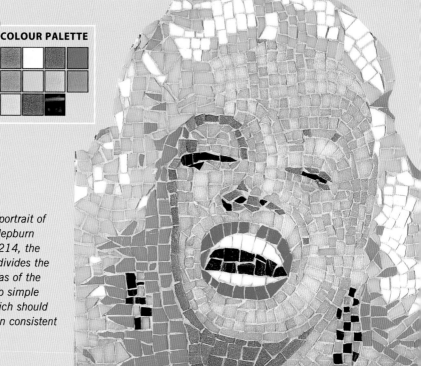

FLAPPER GIRL

Rich, bronzed tiles create the weight of the hair in this portrait. The more subtle skin tones give a contrasting subtlety and depth to the face and neck. The mouth, cut from a square of four red tiles, works like the full stop at the end of the sentence – so be prepared to cut a few tiles to get the shape of the lips absolutely right to give the character of a 1920s flapper.

scale drawing

The drawing has a strong, almost Egyptian feel that you can interpret through a range of colour palettes.

All the jewellery in this piece could be further embellished by including found objects (such as buttons, beads and glass) into the mosaic or adding sequins and diamanté after the mosaic is completed.

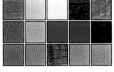

COLOUR PALETTE

GROOVY GIRL

This groovy girl has a 1970s hairstyle and colour theme. Decorate her hair with butterflies or flowers and try different palettes from that period – deep purples, vibrant oranges or acid greens.

COLOUR PALETTE

scale drawing

The darker shades of the girl's hair should be cut and positioned first, using strong shapes to accentuate the curliness of her hair.

STILL LIFE

Still-life mosaics can be anything from simple, homely motifs through to the challenge of painting with mosaics. The examples on the following pages include strong abstract motifs that take real-life objects as a starting point, through to naturalistic studies that show the possibilities of mosaic as a pictorial medium.

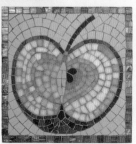

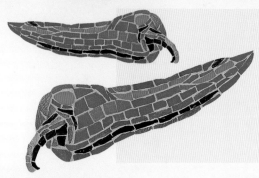

FRUIT BOWL

A simple and exuberant piece, which suggests the natural form of fruits through geometric shapes. Using the squareness of uncut tiles to suggest the form of the pineapple is particularly effective. The hardest part is cutting the circular form of the grapes. You can experiment with different designs for the bowl – a simple white bowl would work just as well as more complex patterns.

scale drawing

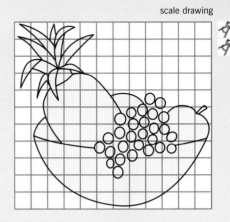

COLOUR PALETTE

A shadow of darker tiles has been added below the grapes to give the piece some depth. To create the appearance of a shadow on a bowl, use darker tones of the colour of the bowl.

CHILLI ON A PLATE

Use concentric ellipses and two bright colours to suggest the shape of the plate, and then red hot, primary colours to make this fiery chilli really stand out against the background.

scale drawing

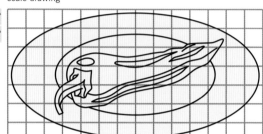

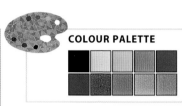

COLOUR PALETTE

You could also cut the baseboard for this piece as a perfect circle, with the design of the chilli centred within it, to make a stand for pots and serving dishes in the kitchen. Either way, mosaic the chilli first, then the plate around it.

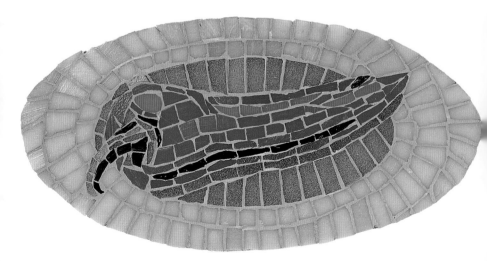

CAKE ON A PLATE

Rather a strange culinary combination – a fruit cake with a chocolate icing – but it looks pretty edible. The plate is created in exactly the same way as in the chilli mosaic on the facing page by drawing and filling two concentric ellipses with contrasting colours.

scale drawing

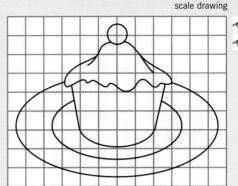

This cake design leaves you free to try any colour combination for the icing and the cake itself.

MIX & MATCH

You could embellish the plate further by using flower motifs or patterns from other chapters of this book.

COLOUR PALETTE

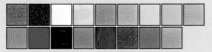

GRAPES AND WINE

This piece relies on the use of carefully selected colours to create a realistic sense of the colour and texture of the real-life objects. The colours chosen for the grapes in particular convey the softness of the fruit under a thin dusting of yeast. Look carefully at how the tiles contour the apples and oranges to make them appear spherical.

scale drawing

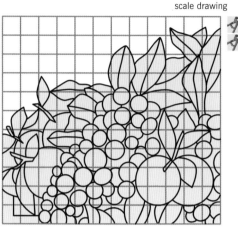

COLOUR PALETTE

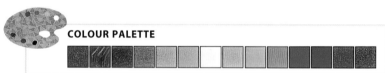

Try to copy how the individual grapes are cut to appear to be in front or behind each other. The choice of grout – here a mid tone – cleverly holds together the background objects, whilst accentuating the separateness of the darker grapes in the foreground of the picture.

LEMON

Cross-sections of fruit have great decorative potential. Here the direction of the tiles, flowing outwards from the centre, mimics the flesh of the segments. This piece would work equally well with deep-coloured tiles defining the outline of the fruit and the edges of the segments.

scale drawing

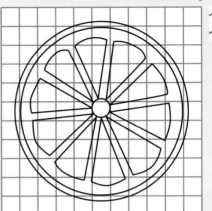

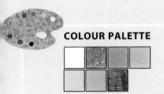

COLOUR PALETTE

Change the colours to make slices of oranges and limes. A combination of these would work well as a kitchen border.

APPLE

scale drawing

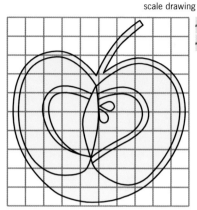

You can almost taste the crispness of this cut apple, in which the softness of the flesh is in contrast to the dark skin and the punctuation marks of the pips. Contouring the inner fill to the shape of the outline and core accentuates the sense of succulence.

COLOUR PALETTE

The cut fruit could be incorporated into a larger still-life piece or intertwined with a serif letter A (see page 130) to make an alphabet study for a child's bedroom.

PEPPER

This red pepper with its lush colours creates an effective but relatively simple piece. As with the previous designs, it has obvious possibilities as decoration for cooking and eating areas, or to incorporate into a cutting board or worktop.

The subtle blending of pearlescent tiles to create the seeds of the pepper contrast well with the heat of the flesh.

This motif could be repeated in the different colours of peppers to create a larger piece – the vivid results achieved by placing areas of red and green together (which are complementary colours) could be exploited in such a piece.

scale drawing

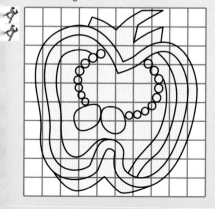

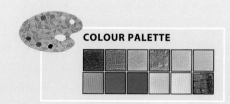

COLOUR PALETTE

PEARS

The drawing for these pears is one of the simplest in this book, yet the finished example shows how the basic ingredients of mosaic – colour and position – can produce a startling result.

scale drawing

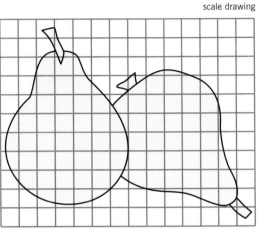

Contour the tiles to follow and strengthen the outline of the pears. Notice how the shadow of one pear helps to sharply define the edge of the other.

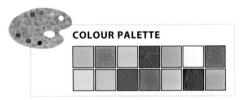

COLOUR PALETTE

The finished palette is quite extensive, but draw from it wisely. Resist the temptation to use white or very bright tiles to create the highlights as these can destroy the subtlety of the final effect.

PIZZA

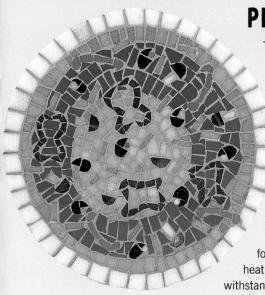

This pizza is ideally suited to be used as a trivet or stand for hot pots and pans to be brought to a dining table. The pizza design works best life-size. The variety of possibilities are as endless as the choice of pizza toppings – this example is full of vegetables, but you could experiment with an extravaganza of seafood and meat toppings.

Vitreous mosaics are ideal for this type of use. They are heat resistant and resilient and will withstand bleaching, scrubbing and scouring (but remember that the baseboard is not oven-safe so never put a mosaic piece like this in an oven). It is wise to use a grey or toned grout to avoid staining.

The pizza can be as complex as you want – combine it with other motifs such as the pepper on page 233.

COLOUR PALETTE

scale drawing

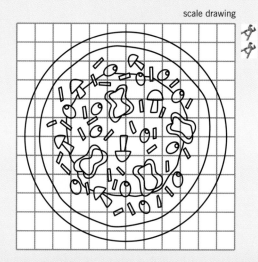

BUILDINGS

Do not be fooled into thinking that buildings with their rectangular or linear shapes provide any less of a challenge to the mosaicist than the other motifs included in this book. You need to pay great attention to the shapes of the bricks and roof tiles, for example, to create realistic effects.

COUNTRY COTTAGE

This is a traditional gingerbread house with window boxes and roses around the door. Care should be taken to make the brickwork and roof tiles regular in size and position; save the embellishments for the floral decoration and windows.

scale drawing

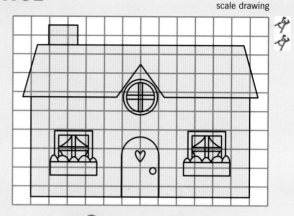

COLOUR PALETTE

Add as much vegetation as you like to the outside of the cottage. Use the flower details on pages 204–205 for inspiration. Alternatively, develop a sequence of cottages, adapting the idea of the Four Seasons series featured on pages 206–209.

CASTLE

The initial idea behind this piece was to create a fairy-tale scene. However, the end result has more of a haunted castle feel. While it is still an effective piece, using warmer colours and some climbing roses rather than skeleton trees would have taken it in the direction originally intended.

scale drawing

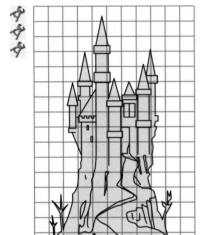

COLOUR PALETTE

Stand back from the piece from time to time to ensure that the shadows and highlights are working effectively, to stop it becoming a silhouette.

TEPEE

This mosaic of a tepee uses patterns from traditional Native American art, arranged in simple, horizontal stripes.

scale drawing

COLOUR PALETTE

Look at books and reference material on Native American art, particularly woven rugs and materials, to find other patterns and colours to use in this design.

BEACH HUTS

scale drawing

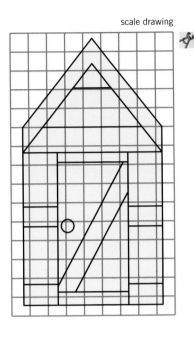

Beach huts are such a popular motif, and these make an ideal beginner's piece as they are cut from simple rectangles – only the circular door handle requires more difficult cuts.

You could extend the series to form a decorative frieze within the wall tiles of a bathroom. Experiment with a sun-bleached colour palette. The beach huts would also make an ideal background to use behind a more complex centrepiece mosaic such as the seagull (see page 175).

The making of this piece is shown in detail in the step-by-step instructions in the Basic Techniques chapter, on pages 53–59.

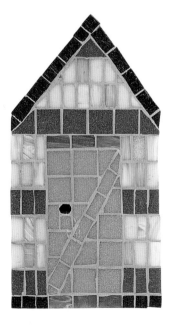
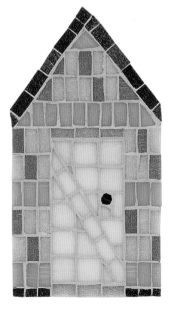
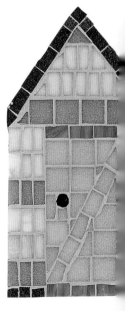

COLOUR PALETTE

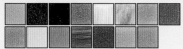

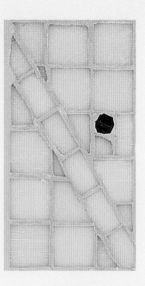

MIX & MATCH

If you wish to add a foreground to the beach huts, try adding some of the shells featured in the Marine Life chapter, on pages 170–173, or bands of sand and sea.

This beginner's piece could be simplified even further by omitting the diagonal detailing from the door.

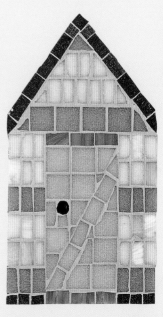

CELEBRATIONS

Festive occasions provide the mosaicist with a welcome reason to create decorative objects of all types to display in their home or to give as presents. On the following pages are motifs for some major festivals which can be adapted and mixed with other designs to create unique and personalized pieces.

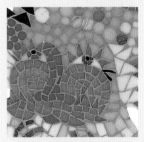

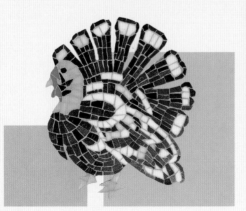

ANGEL AND BIRDS

scale drawing

This design is a copy of a painting my father did for me when I was a child. The original now hangs in my own children's bedroom. I have added to it by making circles to give the sense of curly hair, but I hope I have not lost the sentiment and prettiness of my father's original.

The angel's head is deliberately quite large and slightly out of proportion with her body. This is an important element in achieving the sense of child-like wonderment of the figure.

MIX & MATCH

As a variation, use the fern design on page 202 to provide a gentler, intertwined alternative to the branches.

COLOUR PALETTE

THANKSGIVING TURKEY

Stark black and white with a few hot colours make this a bold motif, unlike the more naturalistic treatments of birds elsewhere in this book. It is a design ideally suited for use in a kitchen, perhaps as part of a splashback or as a trivet or hotplate.

Do the white detail of the plumage first to give a strong shape, then mosaic the turkey's head and claws. Lastly, fill in the black plumage.

scale drawing

Here this turkey has been represented in quite a stylistic way, but you could use a varied blend of tiles to achieve the more realistic effect of pieces like the owl on page 147.

COLOUR PALETTE

scale drawing

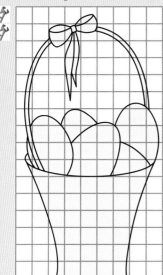

EASTER BASKET

This is a straightforward piece where you can experiment with different tile patterns and colours for the individual eggs.

First, decide which size tiles you are going to use to achieve the weave effect, then draw out each row, curving downwards slightly at the middle to create a three-dimensional effect. You can then draw the downwards columns of the weave, this time curving towards the centre to enhance the shape of the container.

Complete the front edge of the basket, then the eggs in the foreground, before moving on to those behind.

MIX & MATCH

This basket would look just as pretty filled with flowers as a present for Mothering Sunday. See pages 204–205 for flower details.

COLOUR PALETTE

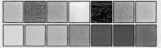

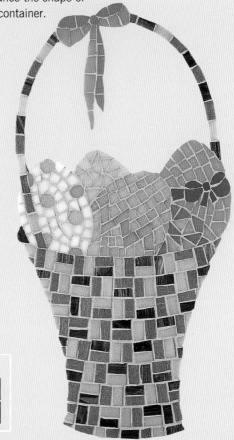

scale drawing

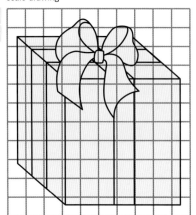

GIFT PARCEL

This parcel is based around a simple, stylized cube. The left side is filled with lozenge-shaped tiles to create perspective. A shadow has been placed around the bow to better define its shape. A label could be added to the parcel, personalized with a name or a heart for a Valentine's day gift.

Start with the bow and its shadow, then work on each face of the parcel separately to keep them distinct.

Instead of stripes, more complex patterns could be used, although you will need to distort these to retain the three-dimensional effect.

COLOUR PALETTE

CHINESE DRAGON

The dragon is a motif that features throughout Chinese civilization. The benevolent dragon signifies greatness, goodness and blessings. Eastern astrologers say that children born during the Year of the Dragon enjoy health, wealth and long life.

There is a lot of detail in this dragon. Establish the black and yellow areas first, particularly the spine on the back, then fill the space in between.

scale drawing

COLOUR PALETTE

FATHER CHRISTMAS

This is a traditional Father Christmas with red nose and cheeks, and sprigs of holly added for interest. In this example the white of the hat band has been cut as circles and the beard as rectangles, to stop similar white areas merging into one – you might like to try reversing these cuts.

The holly sprigs are stylized versions of the leaves. You could add a more realistic version if you wish.

scale drawing

You could add a Christmas greeting to the design to turn it into a plaque to hang in an entrance hall or as part of a fuller decoration for the festive season.

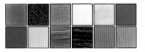

COLOUR PALETTE

CHRISTMAS TREE

scale drawing

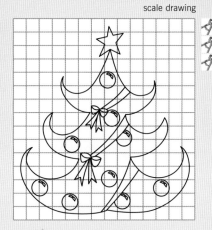

If you have a jigsaw, cut the baseboard out of MDF about 5mm (¼ inch) beyond the outline of your drawing. You can then place eyelets and a picture wire on the back to hang the tree as a festive decoration in an entrance hall or stairwell. Dress the tree to your taste – create little parcels, candles, candy sticks or holly leaves. You could make the tree more natural and similar to a fir tree with straighter, pointed branches and add a trunk if you wish.

In this example the baubles on the tree were created first. Each bauble is based around a central tile, cut to a circle as carefully as you can manage; two outer circles are then placed around this centre. A highlight or reflection is added in each bauble by substituting some light or pearlescent tiles at the same position in the outer circle.

You could add a pot to this design or decorate the tree with small versions of the parcel motif, holly sprigs or Christmas roses.

COLOUR PALETTE

RESOURCES

AUSTRALIA

Flat Earth TileWorks
4 Forth Street
Kempsey, NSW 2440
Tel: 02 6562 8327
www.midcoast.com.au/~vanz/

Metric Tile
38-42 Westall Road
Springvale 3171
Victoria
Tel: 03 9547 7633
www.infotile.com.au/metrictile

Mosaria
311 Colburn Ave
Victoria Point
Qld 4165
Tel: 07 3207 6380
www.mosaria.com.au

CANADA

Interstyle Ceramic & Glass Ltd
3625 Brighton Ave
Burnaby
Vancouver
B.C., V5A 3H5
Tel: 0604 421 7229
www.interstyle.ca

UK

Edgar Udney & Co Ltd
The Mosaic Centre
314 Balham High Road
London SW17 7AA
Tel: 020 8767 8181

Focus Ceramics
Unit 4 Hamm Moor Lane
Weybridge Trading Estate
Weybridge
Surrey KT15 2SD
Tel: 01932 854881
www.focusceramics.com

Mosaic Workshop
Unit B
443-449 Holloway Road
London N7 6LJ
Tel: 020 7272 2446
www.mosaicworkshop.com

Reed Harris Ltd
Riverside House
27 Carnwath Road
London SW6 6JE
Tel.: 020 7736 7511
www.reed-harris.co.uk

Tower Ceramics
91 Parkway
Camden Town
London NW1 9PP
Tel: 020 7485 7192

USA

Hakatai Enterprises
695 Mistletoe Road
Suite C
Ashland, OR 97520
Tel: 541 552 0855
www.hakatai.com

Mosaic Workshop USA
1221 South Burnside Avenue
Los Angeles, CA 90019
Tel: 917 690 4290
www.mosaicworkshopusa.com

Norberry Tile
Seattle Design Center
Suite 221
5701 Sixth Avenue South
Seattle, WA 98108
Tel: 206 343 9916
www.norberrytile.com

Pompei Mosaic Tile
11301 Olympic Boulevard
Suite 512
West Los Angeles, CA 90064
Tel: 310 312 9893
www.pompei-mosaic.com

Tile Specialties
P.O. Box 807
High Springs, FL 32655
Tel: 386 454 3700
www.tilespecialties.com

Wits End Mosaic
5020 South Ash Avenue
Suite 108
Tempe, AZ 85282
Tel: 1 888 494 8736
www.mosaic-witsend.com

INDEX

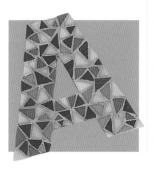

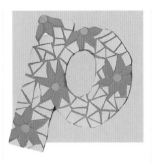

ACKNOWLEDGMENTS

Author's Acknowledgments
I would like to thank my partner, Paul Rutishauser, for his massive help in the writing of this book, my ever-supportive friend, Vera Laing, for all her fantastic grouting, and my mum, who got me started.

The author and publisher would also like to thank Reed-Harris for supplying the mosaic tiles used in the projects. See page 250 for their contact details.

Quarto would like to thank and acknowledge the following artists for supplying pictures reproduced in this book:
page 3 (fish) Judy Wood; page 103 Brett Campbell; page 143 Stewart Hale; page 154 Bea Gullick; page 155 Mary-Kei MacFarlane; page 156 Rosalind Wates; page 157 Stewart Hale; page 158 Robert Field; page 159 Jeni Stewart-Smith; page 160 Robert Field; page 165 Irina Charny; page 173 Jo Letchford; page 174 Jeni Stewart-Smith; page 187 Stewart Hale; page 188 Marcelo José de Melo; page 189 Irina Charny; page 192 Mary-Kei MacFarlane; page 193 Elaine Prunty; page 196 Terry Rudd; page 197 Elaine Prunty; page 216 Robert Field; page 230 Sudarshan Deshmukh; page 231 Jo Letchford; page 232 Jo Letchford; page 233 Jo Letchford; page 234 Terry Rudd.

In addition to the above, some artists are acknowledged beside their work.